# Literary Angles:
## the second year of
# poeticdiversity

from the editors of
poeticdiversity.org

SYBARITIC

PRESS

Published by
Sybaritic Press
8300 Manitoba Street
Suite 107
Playa del Rey, CA 90293
www.sybpress.com

Thank you to Stosh Machek at www.stoshmachek.com for his
contribution to the cover art.

ISBN: 0-9712232-7-0

Printed in the United States of America

First Edition

December 2005

*To those first writers who came and laid the foundations of the Los Angeles literary scene... we are in your debt.*

# Foreward

Dear Readers

Another year has passed, and in your hands you hold the rich bounty of our collective labor: *Literary Angles: the second year of poeticdiversity*.

When I say "us," I, of course mean the contributors. *poeticdiversity* was founded as a way to harness and showcase the incredible diversity of the Los Angeles literary scene, and we are going into our third year of publication. And we'll be around for a few more years, thanks to you all.

As with the previous anthology, this was a collaborative effort. Many thanks go to: *poeticdiversity* contributors' **Aurora Antonovic, David Herrle, Elizabeth Iannaci, Gene Justice, Rachel Kann, Dave Nordling** and **James Pinkerton** for spending many hours carefully reading through each issue, and taking part in the selection process; **Jon Cunningham** and **Deborah Warner** of Sybaritic Press, and most importantly - to all the poets and writers who keep sending us such excellent work.

Enjoy the diversity of *Literary Angles*.

The *poeticdiversity* staff
(Julie Bemiss, Peggy Dobeer, Francisco Dominguez, Reggie Ige, Marie Lecrivain, Laura A. Lionello, Aire Celeste Norell, and Douglas Richardson)

# Table of Contents

## Columns

# Fernando

Fernando
The best Dodger on the mound
Since Koufax and Drysdale.
A finisher, you needed no bullpen,
You had all the answers
Written on the ball.
You were the truest Dodger.
At nineteen, with no English,
Throwing a pitch that no one could
Understand,
Throwing from the deepest blue,
Through the sweat shops,
The day workers at the corner,
Through the ghosts of the Ravine
Whispering in the dugout
As the chant of your name,
Starting in the bleachers,
Rose with your eyes
To the clouds.

# Forgetting to Fill Up in Saskatoon

We ran on empty for an hour,
three boys in a borrowed car,
miles away from anywhere
but these dead farm towns,
without street lamps or oil.

Just burnt out gas stations
and the low moans of cattle
shifting in the dark.

Dry as December, we coasted
all the way home, whispering prayers
and holding our breath as if to lighten
the load till the faint lines of the city
rose at the edge of our view,
like the far off fires of a familiar shore,
and we pulled ourselves in
as weary men, tired of the sea.

(Previously published in *Prairie Poetry*, Dec. 2003)

# What the Lizard Knows

My cat catches mice and lizards
in the brush behind my house.
She carries them in her mouth
across the patio, to the back door,
then lies beside them
looking the other way.
A mouse will hunker motionless
for some instinctive interval,
then try to dart away.
I doubt any have survived.

Lizards are different.
One lizard the cat brought home,
one that was now tailless,
turned and faced my cat—
less than a foot away
and a hundred times its size—
and spread its jaws wide open
in what must be a fearsome display
to ladybugs and gnats.
A lizard must know
that the part of it that's easiest
for others to grab onto, to break off,
is the easiest part to let go of,
and, in time, renew.

When I cower before things half my size—
cold words,
broken promises,
treacherous smiles—

It is because I have forgotten
what even the lizard knows.

(Previously published in *RATTLE* 1995)

# Hamlet's Country Club

Dave Law opened his notebook. The words scribbled down a list read: sulfur, horse's leg on the right, chicken's leg on the left, missing woman.

He removed his car keys from the ignition and exited the car. He looked up the small dirt road ahead. Hamlet's Country Club rested atop the hill. It was a steep climb, but Dave figured he'd walk off his lunch. He kept burping on his drive to the country club. Thai food never seemed to agree with him, but he always said,"I can't live without it!"

He fixed his suit and began to trek up the hill. The clouds formed an ominous backdrop. It was going to rain before sundown, and if Dave were to catch any clues, especially any scent of sulfur and print traces, he'd have to hurry. Halfway up the hill, he started working up a sweat. The wind rushed through the golf course, brushing the trees and greenery back and forth, but the air remained humid.

Dave finally made it to the top. He took a deep breath, looked around and spotted a few empty beer bottles strewn about the parking area. Around the building were a few overfilled trash bins surrounded by flies and many tire tracks on the ground.

He walked over to the building. There appeared to be no one on the premises. He checked for unlocked doors, but found none. He peered into a window. The tables inside still had numerous trays with food, and paper cups filled with liquid on them. There were cutlery and used napkins on the floor. The walls were covered with decorations, and even the dj's equipment was still inside with numerous boxes of LPs stacked nearby.

Loud thunder sprung from the sky and the wind picked up. Dave walked away from the building, still looking around. As he passed by the side of the building, he saw a used condom dangling from a bush. He shook his head and continued his inspection. He kept fixing his hair as the wind ran through it.

Ten minutes passed. A second crash of thunder resonated through the area. The windows trembled slightly. When he didn't find anything out of the ordinary, he decided to widen his search.

Something on the ground caught the corner of his eye.

He walked toward it, then bent down for a closer look. In the middle of the parking area, seemingly lost among countless tire tracks, he found a print; an animal print.

He reached out with his hand to inspect the track, when he heard a rustling sound in the bushes behind him.

"Who's there?" Dave inquired.

There was no answer. The sound grew

louder.

Dave slowly stood up while the wind entered the sides of his suit jacket, lifting them it up.

"Come on out, whoever you are!" Dave commanded.

The source of the noise revealed itself.

"A donkey?" Dave murmured, as faint rays of sunlight crept from behind the gray clouds to shine down on Hamlet's Country Club.

The donkey approached Dave, cautious, but brave. It appeared to be hungry. Dave, surprised at the donkey's approach, looked beyond to the trail of footprints the animal was leaving behind.

A slight shadow formed beside the animal. The donkey slowly continued to approach, while Dave stood still, watching the donkey.

Suddenly, the sunlight shifted and caught Dave's shadow. The donkey, aware of the change in light, stopped. The man standing in front of the animal revealed an enormous wingspan. The donkey stood frozen as the wingspan's shadow began to flutter furiously. The donkey's eyes widened, as thunder sprung from the sky--then turning, it ran off.

Dave watched the animal disappear. As he did, he noticed a large barn in the distance, down below, past the golf courses. The wind picked up speed. The skies cleared, and more sunlight began to appear. He turned, and faced the print on the ground. Using his foot, he erased the print he'd found among the tire tracks.

"Looks like you tried to trick me into thinking you'd bring rain," he whispered, glancing at the sky while his foot moved back and forth, mixing the dirt on the ground.

# My Life

My name is Erik Haber and I was born in the past. I come from a lower-upper middle class family struggling to be average. As a young child all I ever wanted out of life was a toy dump truck, that was all... I never got it. Sure, my father tried to console me by bringing home real dump trucks, but I couldn't be fooled. I can fondly remember saying to him, "Dad, those are not toys!"

In school I had great difficulty because as a kid I suffered from numerous philosophical ailments. I remember one day in class, raising my hand and saying, "I don't get it," and the teacher asking, "What part?", to which I replied, "Just in general." Soon after that the "system" labeled me "existentially challenged" and I had to take special classes to be convinced that I really existed...it didn't work. As you may imagine, all this led to a sort of estrangement from my peers, as no one wanted to hang around with a boy who finger-painted quotes of Jean-Paul Sartre and Albert Camus. In order to deal with the ensuing loneliness I created an imaginary friend, George, in whom I could confide, but eventually it turned out that I was George's imaginary friend. Needless to say, when I finished high school I was supremely confused.

My father worked for a construction company, where he received a great benefit package and, of course, access to plenty of free dump trucks. He wanted me to follow in his footsteps but I rebelled- I went to work for a destruction company, where I had access to plenty of free explosives and subsequently felt sufficiently empowered to ask him kindly not to try to run my life. These were relatively good times for me, as destroying stuff sort of gave me a sense of purpose and belonging. But because I had a deep desire to exercise my restless intellect, and because there were still many drugs I hadn't yet tried, I decided to go to college.

Initially in college I was a physics major, and I liked that because I was interested in questions like "Just what is the magnetic field around a closed circuit?" and "Just how much THC per unit volume is there in a cloud of marijuana smoke?" My enthusiasm in this field soon led me to a high-profile internship with NASA developing the world's first anti-gravity bong. But despite this being a cause I could really get behind, I quickly became stifled by the 9-to-5 grind. In addition, being a physics major who loved to smoke pot, I soon realized that I couldn't efficiently do both, so I would just have to quit... the physics. And it was then that I had a profound realization: I didn't ever want to have a job again.

So, based on this revelation, I changed my

major to English Lit. After barely graduating, I
took up yoga and meditation, and began
pondering questions like "What is God?" and
"What is Love?", and "How can I ever answer
either one when all I'm concerned with is my
stinkin' navel?" And that brings me to the
present, where my destiny is starting to become
clear: Perhaps all hope for a life bound by
practicality and tradition are dashed, that I'll
forever be a wanderer and a ponderer, and that
I'll always wonder just what it is that will
ultimately bring about love and order in the
world. And so now, here I am before you, doing
this...

# Werewolf

Those other twenty-nine days
when the moon taunts you
sometimes just a sliver

those twenty-nine days
when you're not on all fours
with flesh in your mouth

when you're not a monster
Do you make friends with the people
see their movies

Talk with them in public like
you think you're people
How about a human girlfriend

Does she wonder
what happens to you that one night
Are you two in sync

Every time there's a full moon
it's her time of the month
doesn't even come over

Never notices the missing clothes
the dirt on your fingers
the guilt in your eyes

Do you eat salads at restaurants
baby greens with a pleasant gorgonzola

For godsakes, how do you pay for it all?

Employment? You?
What if your boss needs you to work that one night?
There's no one else

What do you do?
He's got a file on you
reads the news

One day, when the moon is big
he'll put it all together
point his human finger at you

Can you already taste this?
Just before the fear takes him
before you open your mouth

he'll get on his knees
beg you
make him live forever

13

# When I Lie

I'd like to have that wide-eyed look,
empty eyes like the ABC at 6 newswoman
with the stiff blond hair-sprayed hair
who has the mask that was frozen in time
by some catastrophe
so she couldn't stop announcing them
one after the other, her voice like a steel trap
When I lie, I'd like to hold the universe perfectly still,
not jostling anything, keeping the status quo, poker face
When I lie I wouldn't see the stack of cards,
all falling in a ripple, catching me up,
tiny sounds echoing in my ears
When I lie, I'd rather not flush or sweat, skin clammy,
I'd just keep it smooth, even,
no one knowing my dark inside
When I lie I'd like it to be like a poem,
one full of places I've never been,
people I could never be,
songs I never sang,
loves I never spoke of,
a lie that might be true

# Sweet

I remembered spattered raindrops on a picture window pane on a gray day. I want to talk about a girl: a sweet girl. We met a few years before the "Changes," before the end of the known world. We were both caught in a waiting game. We became friends.

My life was chiaroscuro. I've never lost the vanity of being aware of how the light portrayed me, even through the Changes. Strange times: time without leaders because everyone in the world had stopped following; time without invasive corporations because everyone began to mind their own business; time without crime because there were no laws to enforce, and time without romance because we had all, in our way, been exposed.

I appreciated the company of a woman who was beautiful, worldly, and articulate, but we were not lovers. I thought she was sweet, and sweet is tangible, and something about that quality turned me off. I would turn my face to my friends, just so, to make my point, and talk longingly of some lover I could take for granted, but I knew they were vain words. I needed someone who could arouse my curiosity and anger, someone who could allow me to throw caution to the wind. That is the way it has been with love with me. With her was all the semblance of what I claimed to want. I knew just what to expect. I saw it. Our friends saw it. She was genuinely attracted to me. But in spite of all of the persuasion and all the hints and all the invitations, I did not venture into her. I refused to be led.

I had left town for a while and I hadn't seen her. It had been raining like the day that I met her, but it had stopped in the evening, so I biked to the grocery store. I wandered over to the meat case. My fingers pressed the flesh of a rack of beef ribs, crinkling the cellophane. I turned around and she was standing in the aisle less than two feet from me. It was disconcerting because she didn't seem to recognize me. I wasn't totally sure if it was her. She looked unnatural, or supernatural. It was as though someone had made a perfect likeness of her, staring there wide-eyed at nothing, as if merely presenting herself to be looked at. I didn't want to be rude, if it was her, but I didn't want to look like an idiot if it wasn't.

I turned my head beneath the fluorescent lights to an angle that brought out my features unmistakably, but when I glanced back in her direction, she had disappeared.

I left without buying anything. I was a little shaken up by the encounter. If it had been her then she was nothing like I knew her. There was something before her that I could not fathom. I was bemused, and more than a little intrigued by this new facet.

16

I unlocked my bike and turned to leave. She was back, standing right in my path. This time she was looking right at me, with an intense and unreadable look in her eyes. It was deliberate, but not desire.

Still not sure, I ventured, "Hi. Are you lost?"

"You're sweet," she said.

There was nothing behind her but pitch-black darkness.

# Artifact

The carpenter is building a simple garden bench.
He uses a slab of redwood nearly three inches thick,
Shaped like the state of Arkansas,
With a stripe of white running along the angled side.
The bench legs are cut from the straight side of
the slab.
Two pieces are glued together to make each leg.
Each leg fits into a dado cut into the underside
of the bench
And must be carefully cleaned up with a chisel.
As the carpenter works the wood, he notices
several things:
The wood is old and dry.
It easily yields to the chisel,
Neither checking or splintering.
There appears to be some figuring on the surface,
Which will give the appearance of waves
Once the seat is oiled.

As the carpenter clears the dados, he
Remembers that the man he bought the slab from
Estimated that it was perhaps seven hundred
years old.
When this slab was a part of a tree
And that tree was just a sapling on a hillside,
In the northwestern part of a country that had not
Been claimed or named by any foreign man,
Europe was extricating itself from the yoke of
Ignorance known as the Dark Ages and straining
Toward the Renaissance.

When this sapling became a tree,
It would still be centuries before
Anyone would conceive of cutting it down,
Much less contemplate making a piece of it into
a bench.
While this tree grew skyward, nations appeared
and collapsed,
Humans acted out their follies, rising and falling
According to the whims of fate.
Countless armies have faced off against each other.
Philosophies, ideals, and ethics have come and gone.
Nearly half of modern history occurred
While this tree grew quietly, undisturbed, in a grove
Somewhere in the northwestern corner of America.

There is a certain, unstated holiness in this moment
Where a man, the maker and breaker of things,
turns a simple
Piece of wood into a thing of beauty, to be
appreciated
And to bear witness to the wonder of this
artifact of nature's glory.

19

# Fighting the Bulls

Four-year-old Avi, the kid who sings at the top of his lungs instead of talking, is at it again. *"I am Avi, I am Avi! You are the people, you are the people..."* It's his own made-up melody, but it resembles Diana Ross's *Baby Love*, which even Avi's father is way too young to remember. *"You are the people, people, people in my shul, shul, shul!"* Avi is standing beneath the flaming red bougainvillea that separates his apartment building from T.J.'s. *"Now everybody listen – to my voice, to my song."* The kid bobs back and forth as he sings, the way grown up Orthodox Jews do when they pray. One of the lonely alley cats rubs up against his pant leg, but Avi doesn't break his concentration. *"Listen and be quiet, be quiet to yourself."* He closes his eyes and holds his second finger to his rosy-red mouth, "Shhhhhh!" Then he blasts away in Hebrew: *"Va-ani tefilati lecha, Adonai, et ratzon!"*

Off into one of his singing trances, Avi doesn't notice his sixteen-year-old neighbor, T.J., standing on his balcony in boxer shorts staring at the clouds and drinking orange juice, his brown beard and long wavy brown hair a tangled mess. T.J. lives with his mom and dad in the building next door to Avi, but not in Avi's world. He looks down at the ecstatic singing tot who's dressed in a size four three-piece suit identical to a man's and wonders what kind of psychic earthquake will finally come along to crush the kid's puffed-up sense of himself. Before T.J. got whacked by the Hollywood poseurs, he felt just as powerful as little Wonderboy down there—powerful enough to believe he could make his father's dreams materialize.

But the little kid looks good, no doubt about that. Avi's silk tie is knotted perfectly, not like the baby clip-ons most little boys wear. And he wears his wide-brimmed black hat that is exactly like his father's as if he deserves the respect it usually brings. T.J. has seen how Avi's blonde curls and rabbi-brown eyes melt hearts. His bravura voice is another story. He's been singing since before he could walk, and the kid's got Pavarotti volume going for him big time. It was cute for a while, when he was a toddler and the songs were mere muffled words and you couldn't help but admire the lilting, perfect pitch melodies coming out of his baby boy mouth. But at four, he already needs a music hall to contain the voice that he refuses to rein in.

*"VA'ANI TEFILATI LECHA, ADONAI, ET RATZON!"*

"Hey—cut it out down there! Can't you make that kid shut up?" The neighbor whose window is closest to the bougainvillea slams it shut.

"Aviram, quiet! People are still sleeping!" His mother calls down from their upstairs window,

21

making a stab at quieting her son, knowing it's as futile as trying to silence the squawking crows. For Avi, every day is an occasion to belt it out, no matter who the hell is sleeping.

"VA'ANI TEFILATI LECHA, ADONAI, ET RATZON!"

From the other planet of his balcony, T.J. can tune out the kid's loud singing if he wants to. Living in such close proximity to your neighbors you either get riled or wall yourself off. Avi is just one of the hordes of Orthodox kids who tear around on their scooters and tricycles and drip ice cream all over T.J.'s speed bike that's chained to the straggly palm tree between the two apartment buildings. This morning, though, Avi's mini-man suit and cocky little macho voice piss T.J. off. What makes baby rabbi so damn sure he commands the world? And when's he gonna fall off that perfect little throne of his?

"VA'ANI TEFILATI LECHA, ADONAI, ET RATZON!"

"Shut up! It's Saturday morning!" Another neighbor slams his window shut, startling the stray cat who's napping near the flowerpots.

"Hey don't worry, Avi," T.J. mutters sarcastically to the singing midget as he heads back inside his apartment. "They used to tell Bob Dylan to shut up too."

"So, T.J., how many miles are you up to?" Avi's mom is folding laundry on the steps of their apartment. She's the first one up except for T.J., who couldn't sleep and is headed to Roxbury Park for a Sunday morning run.

"Only about ten or twelve. No big deal."

"Sounds impressive to me. Are you on the track team?" Avi's mother is a Torah teacher at the Orthodox high school for girls down the street, and his father is a rabbi at a small *shul* on Pico. They're both in their twenties and already have three kids.

"Nah — not my thing."

T.J. thinks Avi's mom is one of the cheeriest women on the block. She radiates a hard-to-believe but not-fake contentment. Unlike the other over-worked Orthodox moms with big families, she hardly ever yells at her kids or loses her temper. T.J. wonders what her secret is, because whatever it is, she hasn't shared it with her husband, who wears a permanent expression of exasperation. Except when he's listening to Avi sing. And then his face breaks into pure joy bordering on idol worship.

T.J. has no idols. He has distrusted pop culture since he was two, when he figured out that TV was just something little kids and their dads sit in front of so they can fall asleep.

23

Because his dad has always been involved with rock music and films, T.J. became jaded by it all at an early age. He outgrew rap at nine, action films at ten, MTV at twelve.

But that didn't mean he completely divorced himself from Hollywood. It was always a father-and-son thing for him and Rafe to read *The LA Times* box office tallies together each morning, assessing the fickle state of the industry. For as long as T.J. can remember, his family has been waiting for one of Rafe's scripts to sell so that they can finally buy a house. But T.J. realized years ago what a long shot his father's dream was—even though they live only blocks from where movies, music and celebrities are developed and packaged. While Pico-Robertson is its own foreign country, it's in the shadow of Fox, MGM, Sony, and ICM, where T.J. has gone with his dad on numerous occasions to drop off scripts that might have been their ticket out of P-Ro.

T.J. tried to earn that ticket for his dad last year. He wrote a script—a teen drag-race movie, exactly what Hollywood was craving at the time. At fifteen, T.J. pitched it to agents on his own. They loved his concept—but what they really loved was that the script was written by a teenager. *"That'd be a killer marketing hook,"* was their general take. T.J. took more meetings than his father ever had in all the years he'd been

24

sending out scripts. But in the end the fat cats nixed T.J. in favor of a well-known entity. No big surprise.

Now T.J. never goes to movies, shuns radio and TV, and has time for only three musicians: Dylan, Mozart and Lou Reed. He finds kids his age naïve for getting sucked in by the copycat media and the whole *you-can-make-your-dream-come-true-if-you-try-hard-enough* thing.

*"HE NAY MAH AH TOV, SHEVET ACHEEM GOM YAHAD!*

*"HE NAY MAH AH TOV, SHEVET ACHEEM GOM YAHAD!"*

T.J. is in the middle of a final stretch as Avi strides solemnly down the stairs crooning his tune in full voice.

*"HE NAY MAH AH TOV, SHEVET ACHEEM GOM YAHAD!"*

"Ever heard of Mozart?" T.J. shouts, in order to be heard above the booming voice that's giving him a second-degree headache. "He started out real young too, just like you." Avi's mom grins, flattered by the comparison, even though T.J. said it mockingly. Avi looks past them and heads for his pulpit beneath the bougainvillea.

*"HE NAY MAH AH TOV, SHEVET ACHEEM GOM YAHAD!*

*HE NAY MAH AH TOV, SHEVET ACHEEM GOM YAHAD!"*

Avi doesn't hear anything but his own voice when he sings. He loves how it echoes in his head and in his chest so that he feels like he's flying. When he opens his mouth and the songs come out, he doesn't hear his parents or the neighbors or the teenager boy T.J. with the big brown beard and the long, wiggly hair that falls all into his face, the boy who's running away now.

*"HE NAY MAH AH TOV, SHEVET ACHEEM GOM YAHAD!"*

* * * *

On his way to Roxbury Park, T.J. runs past the landmarks of his childhood. Golden Apple Comics where he graduated from Ghostbusters to Ninja Turtles to Anime when he was four, six, nine; Beverlywood Bakery, the only non-kosher bakery in P-Ro, where he and his friends bought sprinkle cookies on their way home from elementary school; King David Computers where the Israeli owner cursed T.J.'s dad under his breath for being severely technologically challenged; and The Milky Way, Steven Spielberg's mom's fancy kosher restaurant where T.J.'s parents took him to celebrate his first meeting with a Hollywood agent. All the kids T.J. used to hang out with in P-Ro have long since moved to better neighborhoods, but

26

T.J. doesn't mind that he's still here among the flashy lower class Persians and the argumentative Israelis and the always-celebrating-some-holiday-or-other Orthodox Jews. The wackiness of his neighborhood makes him forget the strain of putting up with the irrelevant propaganda they try to stuff him with at high school and the eager-to-suck-it-right-up kids he has to fake getting along with.

Turning onto a residential street, T.J. jogs past small and medium-sized stucco houses with *sukkahs* in their yards — in celebration of the holiday *Succot*. Some of the little huts are more elaborate than others — ranging from simple plastic-sheeted walls and paper daisy chain decorations to wood constructed shelters with fancy purple velvet walls, Chinese lanterns, Christmas tree lights, fold-out Jewish stars, and multi-colored paper mache fruits. T.J. thinks it would be fun to eat in a *sukkah* for a week if you were a kid. Like a cross between camping out and living inside a giant Christmas tree. Once a long time ago, when he was five or six, his mom decided they should have a sukkah on their balcony — *"Hey, why can't we celebrate the journey to the Promised Land like everyone else around here?"* — and they made a makeshift hut, decorating it with handmade cut-outs of pears and pineapples and bananas. T.J. remembers spending a rainy day coloring all the decorations with his mom and being excited about having a picnic in their little *sukkah* on the balcony that night. But during their first dinner under it, the know-it-all little girl down the street whose dad is a rabbi from Ireland of all places strolled by to tell them that it wasn't a real *sukkah* because for a real one you needed four walls, and theirs only had three. Like that's gotta be a big deal, T.J. thought. It's an ancient symbol, not some architecture assignment. She was probably just pissed because she knew T.J.'s dad isn't Jewish. In fact, he's an Italian Catholic Buddhist. But T.J. figured his dad knew as much about God as Little Miss I'm-a-Real-Jew-and-You're-Not's father anyway. Big shot rabbis, big shot Hollywood agents—it's all the same con. They rule the game even if some outsider comes along with the deeper stuff.

At Roxbury Park, T.J. sees some kids from school but avoids them by doing his laps around the outer edge of the park where they won't notice him. Where is Buddha anyway, when you need him to make you invisible?

\* \* \* \*

On his way back from the park, T.J. spies Avi running around the apartment courtyard with nothing on—a jarring departure from the

28

dressed-to-kill rabbinical look. Avi is giggling and singing and taunting his mom as she's trying to catch him into a towel. He darts in and out of the patches of sunlight, playing tag with his shadow.

"Did you make ten miles?" Avi's mom treats T.J. almost like an equal. Actually, she's only eleven years older than he is, as T.J.'s mom pointed out once. Which T.J. thinks is pretty bizarre. She's so mom-like he can't picture her ever being sixteen. She has a young face and pretty green eyes, but the headscarves and long skirts don't help.

"Actually a bit further today... Hey Avi, where's your clothes?"

Avi doesn't look at T.J. but stops his giggling and running around long enough to sing out in his booming tenor voice, "THE RABBIS ARE NAKED!"

T.J. and Avi's mom look at each other, wondering where the other nude religious leaders might be hiding.

"I SAID, THE RABBIS ARE NAKED. DIDN'T YOU HEAR ME?"

Avi's delivery is as close to Wagnerian as a preschooler can get.

It has never occurred to T.J. to take Avi's whole life-is-an-opera thing more seriously. Ever since Avi's family moved in, they've melted into the crazy P-Ro environment and

29

T.J. has taken "the voice" for granted. But now he wonders why Avi never talks without singing — or if he's got some kind of emotional problem.

"Rabbis plural?" Avi's mother says, looking to T.J. for his input.

"Maybe it's the royal we," he offers.

"Hm...You think I have a little monarch on my hands?" She shoots T.J. a conspiratorial smile.

Avi sneaks in and snatches the towel from his mom but instead of wrapping up in it begins to do a kind of bullfighter's dance, using the towel as a prop. *The rabbis are naked, are naked, are naked!* Now his tune is less opera and more eighties pop.

"The rabbis are going to have a time out if they don't give their mother the towel by the time I count to three. See ya, T.J."

T.J. takes the hint and walks off, pondering the connection between naked rabbis and bullfighters.

"One...two...I mean it, Avi — Oh, hey, T.J.! You doing anything for dinner?

"You wanna eat dinner with us in the *sukkah*?"

T.J. turns to see Avi bullfight-dancing with his towel. His family and Avi's don't really socialize beyond neighborly conversation, so he's a bit thrown by the invitation. Avi now expands his dance with a chorus of the ever-popular…

*"HE NAY MAH AH TOV, SHEVET ACHEEM
GOM YAHAD!"*

"Sure."

"THREE! Okay, Avi. Get upstairs. See you at
six, T.J.!"

\* \* \* \*

Avi's family's *sukkah* is built on the small
stucco balcony of their upstairs apartment.
Funky but functional. The paper decorations
made by Avi and Simchi with their mother's
help—crayoned fruits and Hebrew letters with
glitter and sequins stuck on—give it a homey
look. And the palm fronds forming the roof
could definitely let the stars shine through—as
*sukkah*-building rules dictate—if there were any
in L.A. But eating in it is a more serious affair
than T.J.'s casual *sukkah* experience as a six-
year-old. Before they sit down to dinner, the
family recites a prayer as they all take turns
ritualistically washing their hands. Then Avi's
father says a series of blessings over the food
and gives a lengthy explanation to T.J. about the
basis of the holiday.

T.J. pretends to be interested even though
he's floating above the surface of the rabbi's
words. Tuning in just long enough to hear the
phrase, *wandering Jews*, T.J. thinks about how

31

little he's wandered in his life. P-Ro is the only home he's known and his limited travels have been with his parents—aside from a few backpacking trips with his cousins. He wonders how it would feel to wander far away from everything that's familiar. To lose who you think you are and morph into someone you don't know.

Seated between Simchi, who is whispering five-year-old secrets into his ear, and baby Esther, who's baby-talking to him in a voice loud enough to rival Avi's while throwing bits of food down from her high chair, T.J. barely notices Avi until he breaks into song—which he does in between mouthfuls. "*Celebration in the sukkah, celebration, celebration. Eat with us, sing with us, eat with us, sing!*" Another made-up melody, probably based on some old Lionel Ritchie song.

T.J. realizes that Avi is checking him out to make sure he's listening, so he tries to nod approvingly at the appropriate moments. *Sing, celebrate, dance around naked—what does it all amount to anyway?* T.J. asks silently. *If you only knew how all that little kid joy is going to come crashing down on you in a few years you wouldn't have so much to sing about—on Shabbos or Sukkot or any other fucking day.*

"*You will sing, you will sing, you will sing a Sukkah song.*"

The persistent big-little voice, the demanding trio of kids, the claustrophobic dinner table— *And why did I accept this invitation?* T.J. asks himself, wondering if he'll make it through the evening without keeling over. *Maybe it's time to focus on some grown-up conversation.*

"So, what did the Jews back in Jesus' day have against him?" T.J. asks Avi's parents, who are enjoying the momentary freedom from their children, thanks to him. Avi's dad gets a pained expression as he passes T.J. the *challah*. Then he gives his wife a *Why do I even have to explain these things?* look.

"There were a lot of men like Jesus then, claiming to have all the answers," the rabbi tells T.J.

"But he did have a lot of good answers, didn't he? About love being more important than all the rules?" T.J. remembers hearing this from his dad, the Catholic Buddhist.

"Because God loves us we follow His rules," Avi's father answers, with his characteristic unruffled exasperation. "It's about showing love for God. Doing what He commands."

"*Hm...Yeah, I guess that makes sense,*" T.J. says, although it makes no sense to him at all. *How the hell does anyone know what God commands? Because some old guys wrote it down thousands of years ago and called it a Bible, that's supposed to be the deep dark truth?*

33

"I like the question, though, T.J." Avi's mom passes him the casserole of spicy meat, beans and stewed fruit. "Jesus was definitely spreading new ideas about how to practice our religion."

Avi's father rolls his eyes.

"We'll have to do a bit more studying about Christianity, won't we, honey," Avi's mom continues, " — so we can discuss this further with T.J.?"

Avi's dad shoots his wife an *in-my-next-lifetime* look and helps his daughter spoon out more casserole. "Take more meat, Simchi. Don't just eat the fruit."

"My dad told me the reason Jesus went against the whole kosher thing was that it's more important what comes out of your mouth than what goes into it. Did you ever hear that?" T.J. has no idea why he has brought this up — *Am I being an idiot or just a punk?*

Avi's father gets the pained look again. "It's not a question of either or — Simchi take more meat — both are important."

T.J. appreciates the rabbi's short answers — unlike his parents who turn every dinner table discussion into a prime time debate.

"*HA-VA, V-NEEV SU-KAH!*
*BA TE-SHEV K-MO MAL-KAH!*"

"A song he learned for *Sukkot*," Avi's mom explains to T.J. He's now trying to diplomatically pay attention to Simchi, who has just asked him why his hair's in a pony tail; pick up the baby's cup, which she keeps throwing down; while still listening to Avi's song and his mom's explanation of it. *Do these people always talk and sing and throw things and ask questions at the same time? Jesus Fucking Christ.*

"HA-VA, V-NEEV SU-KAH!
BA TE-SHEV K-MO MAL-KAH!"

"So how come you never got Bar Mitzvahed? Your dad opposed to it?" The rabbi has decided to help T.J. out and gets up to pick up the baby's cup this time.

"Nah—he would have been fine with it. I'm just not really into organized religion."

"HA-VA, V-NEEV SU-KAH!
BA TE-SHEV K-MO MAL-KAH!"

"You prefer disorganized religion?"

"HA-VA, V-NEEV SU-KAH!"

"Yeah—that's a good one!" T.J. likes the rabbi's bluntness.

"BA TE-SHEV K-MO MAL-KAH!
"BA TE-SHEV K-MO MAL KAAAAH!"

The pre-school lounge singer who won't quit is another story. Isn't it time someone told the rabbi and his wife to consult a child psychologist or a pediatric brain surgeon? What's with this kid? T.J. had thought the dinner would be a mind-freeing break from his caveman ritual—if he weren't here he'd be sealed off in his room listening to the holy three —but Avi is starting to seriously get on his nerves. How do his parents carry on like everything's normal when they're being blasted by a wacked-out, mini-human jukebox they can't turn off?

* * * *

Again T.J. can't sleep. Avi's pumped-up, one-man choir gave him a raging headache that the September heat is making worse. He flings off his bedclothes and heads out to the balcony where at least there's a slight breeze. Pushing the plastic chaise lounge against the outer wall, he goes back inside to get his sheets to block out the apartment lights from next door. Draping the sheets to make himself a little tent, T.J. realizes it's almost a *sukkah*. All he needs is decoration. He heads inside again, grabs some safety pins and an issue of *Martha Stewart Living*, and tears out some artistic close-ups of pears and pomegranates. *Take that, little tyrannical daughter of an Irish rabbi!*

T.J.'s sleep is fitful, but he likes waking up to the noisy crows and Martha Stewart pears.

* * * *

T.J. ignores the taunts at school and walks across the quad in his own righteous fog. His full beard has been growing since he was fifteen so he's used to the Moses label. He knows his wild man hair and bushy Jewish-Italian face intimidate some and infuriate others, and he tells himself he's fine with that.

"Hey, Mo, how's it growin'?"

"Trapped any bugs in there, man?"

T.J. flashes a peace sign and walks past his fellow eleventh graders. He plays his role, they play theirs. *It's all just a dream, a vacuum, a scheme…*as Dylan once put it. He heads for the bench at the far end of the lunch area, sits down and takes a swig from his water bottle.

It's been almost two years since he staked out this spot. Now it's his. No one else dares to intrude — with the exception of Manuel, the janitor who comes by almost everyday.

"How's it going, T.J." he asks now, leaning on his broom with a crooked smile.

"It's going great, how 'bout you?" T.J. says, taking a bite of his sandwich and knowing Manuel can see through his answer.

"I'm doing pretty good, my friend, pretty darn good."

And T.J. can see that he is. *So what's Manuel's red-hot secret? Is he really as fucking content as he seems? Maybe he has a gorgeous wife at home who plays Spanish guitar and serenades him in the nude after work.*

"You sure there's nothing bothering you?"

"Nah—I'm fine."

*Just fine—other than feeling that I can't take one more day of this mindless quiz show—and have nowhere to escape to except my cave and this fucking bench.* Ringing in his head is Lou Reed's *Walk on the Wild Side.*

*DOOT, DA DOOT, DA DOOT, DA DOOT DOOT...*

Last week it was Dylan's *Not Dark Yet,* the week before Mozart's *Piano Concerto #5 in B-flat.*

"You take care now, T.J." Manuel pats him on the back and walks away, and for some reason T.J. feels like a three-year-old whose mom has just dropped him off at preschool. What the hell is happening to him? Is he actually going to break down and bawl in the middle of the lunch area? *Oh, Jesus.*

He gets up from his private bench and throws the barely eaten sandwich into the trash. *Just take a few deep breaths,* he tells himself. *Get it together, brother.* He breathes deeply and forces himself to walk to his next class.

Kids are staring at him funny, but maybe they always do and the fog has just protected him until now. He sees Marina, the pretty Latina girl from his history class who seems sympathetic, as if she might even know what the hell he's suffering from.

*DOOT DA DOOT, DA DOOT, DA DOOT DOOT*

38

*Doot da doot, da doot, da doot doot*
*Doot da doot, da doot, da doot doot*

Lou Reed's riff is softer now, fading away in fact, and in its place is a strange melodic buzzing in T.J.'s head and down his shoulders. It's a sensation that excites him, thrills him — in spite of his exploding brain. *Keep breathing, you're almost to class, Teej.* The buzzing is now a distinct musical phrase in a minor key. T.J. has never heard this phrase playing on his inner soundtrack before — but it's wildly familiar. *Don't lose it now, brother, or you're a goner.* It builds in his head from a buzzing to a blare, and now he feels it through his entire body. He has an intense sensation of excitement, like when he was little and looking forward to his first train trip — all the way to Union Station he couldn't sit still in the back seat of his parents' car because he was so intent on what it would feel like to be racing down the tracks in a shiny silver bullet. It was like a small bird was trapped inside his chest and the wings were part of his own body. Would he fly down the tracks? Would he ever be able to stop?

He sees the door to his classroom and walks in. Then slides behind his desk in the back of his math class and waits for the music inside his head to quiet down. He's breathing weird and the gay kid sitting next to him asks if he's okay. T.J. nods but the sound in his head is building

39

so that he can no longer hear what's going on in the classroom. *Breathe, boy, breathe...*

And then he finally recognizes the music. And he laughs in a way he's never laughed before, from deep in his gut. *Am I sitting in class or am I flying above it?* What he hears, of course, is the ridiculous *forte* voice from Saturday morning: *VA'ANI TEFILATI LECHA, ADONAI, ET RATZON!*

Stroking his year-old beard, he tries to tune-in to all the ancient-sounding words encircling his brain. *VA'ANI TEFILATI LECHA, ADONAI, ET RATZON!* But it's not the words—in fact it's not even the music, as mesmerizing as the melody is. It's the voice—the bravura voice of the defenseless bullfighter. Scared shitless but taunting the beast anyway.

"T.J.—are you with us?" The math teacher has just asked him for the definition of an indistinguishable permutation. T.J. barely hears the question, as if it's been whispered through a long, echoing tunnel.

"No, actually I'm not with you."

The snickering laughter of his fellow students doesn't faze T.J., who doesn't want to interrupt what he's now hearing.

"Well then maybe you shouldn't be here."

*VA'ANI TEFILATI LECHA, ADONAI, ET RATZON!* rumbles through his brain, and T.J. puts every ounce of his being into stifling the loudest laugh he's ever let out.

"Perhaps I shouldn't." He gets up, leaving his books on the desk, and walks out of the classroom. He barely hears the applause that follows him out the door and would never interpret it as praise anyway. As he pushes open the swinging hallway doors to the wild red bottlebrush trees outside, he finally lets the laugh explode.

* * * *

*"Now everybody listen, listen to my birds. Listen to my wind, to my trees, to my bushes."*

Mini-rabbi is still at it, dressed up in proper suit, tie and hat—even though it's not *Shabbos.*

"Hey, Avi." T.J. feels lost as he waves at his little neighbor. He's not used to being home this early on a weekday, and it feels weird. He's been waiting to blow it big time at school. Now he's succeeded without even trying. He made his big exit—the laughing breakdown felt great—now what?

*"VA'ANI TEFILATI LECHA, ADONAI, ET RATZON"*

Avi stops his aria and looks straight into T.J.'s wooly face.

"I don't understand the words, Avi, but I like your voice," T.J. says without an ounce of sarcasm.

41

Avi parts his mouth as if he's about to say something, but words don't come out. Even in the silence, the little kid's fear-defying voice still rings in T.J.'s head. T.J. looks at Avi and sees himself a long time ago, commanding this same patch of torn up grass. In his Ninja Turtle outfit, wooden sword in hand, he was prepared to fight heroically against the fear, the fat cats, even the failures of his father.

*"VA'ANI TEFILATI LECHA, ADONAI, ET RATZON!"*

"I'm with you, Avi," T.J. says. "Let's go fight the bulls."

*"VA'ANI TEFILATI LECHA, ADONAI, ET RATZON!*

*VA'ANI TEFILATI LECHA, ADONAI, ET RATZON!"*

# Photo, Dee Bruce, Age 16, 1949

A young woman, bread
and butter smile, blonde
curls piled around her,
the same pose seen
from Norma Jean in the 40's
when no one knew who
she was. I look

at my mother now,
she is round and shrunken,
with worry lines carved
into her forehead. The woman

in the picture stands straight,
showing a lithe figure.
She is full of the radioactive
glow of youth. There are
no doubts curving her spine.

I could tell you what happened
to her, the children, the divorce,
the demeaning jobs; but I prefer
to think of her like this:
straight and unafraid,
defiant set of sexual taunt
in her heart-shaped face,
taut stomach, dangerous
in high heels.

(Previously published in *Iodine*)

## Forward March

We fought the good fight.
    We stood by the rock and protested.
We were the voices of Iowa City,
    the bodies, not bombs, in New York.

We stood on street corners in the snow.

We prayed and we sang.
    We released our hysteria
And we kept step, kept step,
    in the land of, as yet, unkept promise.

We slurped oysters at Swan's Depot
    and rode the Bart into the city.
We drifted out to sea on shots of tequila,
    and friendly competition,
and when Schnakey's chute refused to open,
    we stood on Mt. Tamalpais, and
watched the lupine bend in the breeze.

We made our peace with nature,
    lifted our hearts, and toasted
the thrill, and the temporary.
    We scraped out the marrow of our bones
and simmered the living juices
    in caldrons of hope and fear.

And we fed on this alchemical soup,

Over and over,
     over the years, and decades.
And it fed our longing,
     and nourished our thoughts.
It shifted our passions,
     and shaped our votes.
It held our dreams,
     and birthed our children.
It noted our shortcomings,
     and remembered our ancestors.
It gave voice to our compassion,
     and reason to our lives;
Reason, beyond art
     and money, and ego, and nonsense.

# After a Period of Brightness, Earth Dims

A porter ant carrying a globe
           of scone has made its way
the length of the window
           and somewhere in the universe
whole civilizations have
           crumbled. Still, no waiter
brings me water. I have tied
           my lavender napkin into
nun's hats and rabbits,
           waved away pitying glances
couples throw at a woman alone,
           and the shadows on the patio
have grown. The newspaper
           says scientists have measured
Earth's luminance by looking
           at the Moon. Its bright
side lighted by sunshine,
           dark side not completely
black. As Leonardo da Vinci deduced,
           it is dimly illuminated
by light reflected from Earth
           bouncing off soot particles,
moisture droplets.
           That it's growing darker
holds a mystery they have yet
           to crack. Outside, the sun visits
the horizon, a pink wind
           has kicked-up, I imagine
the ant has made it to his queen,
           and still, no waiter brings me water.

## Exodus

"O.K., everybody up. We're leaving."
"Everybody up."
"Everybody to the riverside."
Men walked through the streets, calling out in the early morning. The sun was barely above the pyramids and the head of the Sphinx. The camels still dozed in the villages.

"Habiru, Levites, Benjamins. Everybody to the river, please."

It was the day of the departure, everything seemed ready, everyone was packed, and the gifts of the Egyptians had been tucked away with family items.

"Everybody up."
"Rise and shine."
Heads came to windows.
"What's the matter with you?" The gatherers called up to them. "Don't you know what day it is?"

"Don't you know what time it is? Look at the sun. Why so early?"

"Have to be out of here by noon."

"We can't start wandering in the desert an hour later?"

They massed at the edge of the river, a crowd in coats of all colors, tattered garments, and rich silks, with mules and carts and camels. Many carried their whole lives on their backs.

"Do you belong here? We're Benjamins? You don't look Benjamin to me."

47

"I have no idea where I belong, does it matter in the desert?"

"You should be with your own kind."

They will be a stream clogging the roads, a polyglot mass, entirely different from the ancestors who had come as conquerors generations ago, who had ruled Egypt, and who had learned of holy altars and circumcision from their Egyptian hosts.

Troops stood on the sand behind them, defining the space where the dispossessed must assemble. A cadre of escort in tunics with golden sashes, wearing bronze swords, assembled before them.

"We're ready," said a captain of young middle age, tall and well formed, but not heroic, a cousin of the Royal House doing his military service.

"As ready as we'll be," said his lieutenant, crinkling his nose as he looks at the mass they must guide out of Egypt into Semitic lands. Across the narrows. Where in the world will they leave them? A place, they have been instructed, from which they cannot easily return, should the Dynasties once more falter.

Horns sounded over the dark brown marshes. Along the banks there was a quiet mass. Some prostrated themselves, others knelt before bulls, and others raised their hands toward heaven. There was clearly a variety of worship. Some horses of the Guard whinnied impatiently.

Horns sounded again. The foremost struck tents, loaded carts, gathered up children. Commands were given in different tongues to nations that never had one speech. Torches were lit to lead the way in different quarters; black smoke billowed into the brightening morning.

"Well," said the captain, "we'll get them somewhere."

The captain's horse rose on its hind legs, he raised his sword and lowered it, and galloped across the marsh.

It took 40 days for the crossing, each day the marsh was filthier, more glutted with the residuals of departure and despair. Each day the troops moved closer to the sea, tightening the band, diminishing the space of the assembly. When all the exiles crossed, the horses went right to the water and rode patrol along the banks.

Expulsion. Exile. Exodus. Time will pick the words. Beyond the sea were fields more than desert, less than pasture. The motley, mixed, and incoherent mass, not yet a people, more than an idea, moved on, stopping to graze animals when they can, resting at rare green places that remained from the time it had rained there. They came upon small stone or mud hut villages, killed the men and children, took the animals and the women, sometimes occupied the place, sometimes came and went like a pestilence, like a destructive horde. Often they fought amongst each other, always strife between the tribes, the towns, whatever groupings they have come from.

Like the Zodiac, the months of the solar year, later the Apostles, there were twelve major groupings. New groups joined, mixing into one tribe or another. Some tribes fall to history, forgotten. The people who will someday arrive will not be the same who left Egypt.

Near the equinox, the days are long; they approached land arable but not empty. In their chaotic state they could not possibly conquer even a promised land. The captain gave up hope of his own return to Egypt, called them into a vast circle. He walked among them, nodding, smiling, a statesman and a politician. He climbed a platform. He read what he said he has brought down from the mountain.

"I am the Lord, thy God. Thou shalt have no other gods before me."

"Why did he do that," Jahve asked himself, watching the crowds below, "that will only cause trouble."

## for a moment there last thursday

having spent the whole afternoon
in the park reading poetry,
under palm trees that forgave me
my desire for beat sainthood,
where i might wander dizzy from hunger,
picking up lost pens &
sanctifying scraps of paper,
pausing to let the rain dissolve me like litter,
using my empty cranium as a beggar's rice bowl,
wrapped in thrift store holy robes,
excusing myself from the meal table of my mid-life
  ...having spent the whole afternoon
in the park reading poetry,
with nothing more urgent in my ears than
the clack of the old men's dominoes,
where even the siren's sounds entwined
w/the mourning dove's gentle call &
the crow's welcome shriek,
where my focus narrowed down to the poet's
cross-eyed stare thru owl glasses,
above walrus moustache &
under yellow hippie hair, i
had come back down to earth,
landing in glendale  ...&
passing a corporate coffee shop, i
was stopped short by the barbecue-smoke voice &
mash-whiskey-in-a-mason-jar guitar of robert johnson,
dripping like honey out of a beehive stereo speaker
mounted above the coffee shop's entrance
  ...so i lit a cigarette, &

tried to tune out the passing traffic noise,
the hip-hop car stereos, &
the conversation of the 2 teenage armenian girls
sitting nearby at the plastic tables, &
strained my ears upward,
to hear the man who had sold his soul to the devil
to learn to play the blues  ...&
the bees buzzed, &
the cigarette burned, &
the reflection off the coffee shop window,
cut thru my shadow on the sidewalk
like a sunlight butcher knife  ...& i
was full of nothing, & i
was ready for anything

# The Betta Fish

The afternoon sun clasps
its long fingers around
the bowl tilts colors
toward me vermilion,
indigo, amethyst.
The velvet bodice
is a can of gloss paint-
lid freshly lifted.
The chiffon train
a streak of sunset
drawn from mud;
a drop of ink dispersing
red calligraphy, scrawled
on wet paper.

I transfix on the gift
of a main artery-
on its vital surge.

I do not see the violent
sky before thunder.
Nor the cool glass solid
cast a bored shadow.
(Nor the sun stretch
it longingly across
the desk).
Nor the slow rise,
of solitary hunger.
Do not imagine the flash
of wet body breach

and thrash until still.
I do not see the puddle dry,
nor the colors pale.

## Spat

They are fighting in the park again
Yell and scream like wounded banshees
She's the drunker of the two
He throws a bottle

Return fire is jagged rocks
Their camper windshield is smashed
She takes off all her clothes,

dashes into the middle of the street
Cars honk. Men whistle
She is dancing

The two start to yell even louder
She lobs another rock
bursts a parked car's window

Police sirens blare
She dresses. He flags the cops.
The police nod looking stern.

They won't take her without taking him
Owner of the parked car is not to be found
The next morning they are a couple
walking arm-in-arm, giggling.

It is good to know that
I can break car windows
and dance naked with impunity
in Sunland/Tujunga

(previously published in the *SGVPQ # 25*)

# Westlake Park

Yesterday, a cupcake of a park sparkles
with a delicious little lake.
Westlake Park welcomes
hungry ducks and lovers.
We rent small boats
equipped with radios and romance,
putter around the lake in starlight,
kiss to deep purple songs about
skylarks and nightingales.
That was before the lake's name
was changed to honor a war general.
Someone left their cake in the middle
Guys in red bandannas shoot at blue
splattering strawberry icing all over today.

## Your Mouth

I found your mouth in the trash yesterday.
You threw it away again, didn't you? Always
tossing away vowels, pitching sounds and
saliva. When you fall asleep on your notebook
your inking does not bleed blue on the page.

You threw your mouth in the trash and now
your kisses are stretched skin, flat and airless as
Nebraska. "Pucker up," means nothing to you.

All the while your mouth grows lonelier in
the dumpster, eating whatever it can: spoiled
lettuce leaves, rotting eggshells, and
lawnmower mulch. For the love of God, your
mouth is starving and all you can do is stare at
the wall in our den, a wall as flat and pale as
your mouth-less face.

One of these days a stray cat will paw its way
into the dumpster and find your mouth and try
it on for size and sometime around 3 A.M.
you'll suddenly meow.

I'll awake and turn to you and soberly remind
you that you are not a cat, you are my husband,
and even though it is 3 A.M. and you are
meowing, could you please empty the kitchen
trash can, and while you're at it, retrieve your
mouth from the dumpster?

Because the garbage men are coming
tomorrow and I don't know about you, but I
sure as hell don't want to dig through a trash
heap to find your mouth. And if your mouth
ends up in a landfill, you can forget it. You'll

just have to get a new mouth. And I have no idea what our dentist could possibly do about that.

Honey, I love your mouth. I miss it and all of your teeth, your gums, tongue, tonsils, epiglottis, even your morning breath. I miss your lips all over mine. Please, honey. Don't ever throw your mouth away in the trash again. I promise you tomorrow we will go shopping for floss and Listerine. You'll feel better soon, I promise. We'll read the dictionary together before bedtime. You'll rediscover that sounds and vowels and consonants are not so bad. They can be quite weightless and revelatory. But you must speak them first.

## 5PM Flight

He takes off his ring
sometimes
to hurt,
leaves it tarnished & accusing
near the coffeepot,
where she will see
among the detritus of his
uncaring cohabitation
papers
negatives
toothpicks
socks
sunflower seeds
old, gold icon
the umbilicus.

She wears black as a color and pink leotards,
smoothes SPF 30 on her curious face,
turns up the radio,
pours some juice,
avoids the counter,
orders bowling shoes
through a catalog
and wonders what she has to offer.

She tries on eye shadow and high heels,
wonders how it would feel to be free
unencumbered
emancipated.
She takes a drink

tends her garden
contemplates the 5PM flight to Paris
carries on in spite of his spite
and creates herself a lovely day.

# Escandalosa

The postcard says:
"estuve en Mijas y
pensaba en ti"

I bewitch you like candy
a bad trip
with
lips
hips
I say I love you but it's only a trick
my eyes
tell more lies than those ugly cartoon valentines

I'm escandalosa, nobody's mariposa
My dancing heels laugh
because you pick me the thorny rosa.
Ay!Ay!Ay!
Why did you pick me, the thorny rosa?

## Mining Sierra Nevada Gold

her fingers without flesh
reach
from a grave laid
long ago.
rugged trees once cleared
around a girl,
six, maybe seven;
small number that age difference,
except
when it comes
to how many more weeks
spent hiding
from men who would find her flower,
take her life.
we have something
in common.
this sister's filthy hair
straight,
color of bathwater,
hunches over
a thin back; cracked whole hugging her.
hands held tightly,
we walk
a twisted
path away from the stench,
our steps behind us
hidden
by overhanging branches and corners
with secrets.

## We Are Electric Meat

(excerpt from *Where Are You, Fine-Wine Face?*)

Mona had always loved Beethoven's *Moonlight Sonata*. The patient unrest, the quiet anguish, the to-and-fro tempo.
*Da-da-da/da-da-da/da-da-da/da-da-da/one-two-three/one-two-three/one-two-three/one-two-three.*
Beethoven's music was, as Mona put it, "graceful sadness."

While the *Moonlight* played, Mona imagined Beethoven's precious fingers. She wondered if such an artful man could also be an artful lover. Could he play a woman's body like a piano? She closed her eyes, imagining nimble fingers tapping the moon's mad sadness from her body. *Da-da-da/da-da-da/da-da-da...*

Nero would be back soon. Mona felt profane. She felt like she was teasing the good boy who truly loved her while the bad boy would soon reap her physical rewards. She felt like a Judas-woman betraying the moonlight's only begotten song. Nero had seduced so many women, and Mona knew this fact. He freely shared the most perverse stories with her. However, Mona's attraction only increased. She belonged to a lucky heritage, a chosen harem, but she had unlocked Nero's honesty. She had concluded the heritage, stopped it in its tracks.

"Lucy, I'm hooome!" Nero called in a Desi Arnaz voice. He poked his head in the door and then jumped all the way in, thrusting a dozen roses toward Mona. "Ta-daaaaa!"

Mona turned off the CD player and accepted the flowers. "Aw, thank you, Nero. You're sweet." All her distrust for him drained. "Did you find the wine?"

"Of course I did, legs," Nero boasted through perfect teeth, showing the bottle. "As red as your cheeks will be...after the spanking."

"I'm impressed!" said Mona. A few seconds later she realized the cheeks innuendo. The quick image warmed her. She took the wine and roses to the kitchen. "Want some wine now?" she asked, setting the bouquet and bottle down on the counter.

"Yes!" Nero cheered. He inched his way into the kitchen like a swashbuckler, waving a closed umbrella like a sword. Mona backed up, grabbed the bouquet from the counter, and parried his attack. Something shattered on the floor below her. Mona stepped forward and slipped, crashing face first to the floor. Nero broke caught her body, but her temple hit the leg of a chair. Pain blinded her.

"Mona, Mona!" Nero lifted her to her feet. "You're okay, you're okay. You knocked over the wine bottle and it broke."

Shame replaced the pain. Wine spread like a blush over spanked cheeks. Mona hid her face in Nero's chest, fighting sobs. Her body shook.

She felt wine on her legs.

"You're okay, legs. You're okay. You're just shaken, that's all. Come on, let's go in the other room. Come on."

"I feel so stupid," Mona said. "And that fall. I could have...I could have broken my neck and died."

"No, no."

Nero tried to get her to sit but Mona politely pushed him away. "Yes! I felt like I was going to shatter like that bottle! Look at me! My whole body's shaking like a leaf!"

"Thank goodness leaves don't shatter," Nero joked.

Mona laughed. "They break if they're old," she pouted, returning to his big arms.

"Thank goodness you're far from old, Mona. You're in youth's nucleus."

I hardly know this man, Mona realized. *Despite all the time we've spent together, I really don't know this man!*

"Look at it this way. You almost died back there and I saved your life. I'm your hero."

"Nero the Hero," Mona giggled. She rubbed her temple. "You saved me."

As Nero squeezed her and pecked at her neck, Mona imagined her dead body sprawled on the kitchen floor. She became aroused, thinking of how easily and quickly death happened, how powerful the living are compared to the dead.

"Mona, we all die. That's why we need to have a blast while we're here," said Nero. "We've hardly several decades, and hardly a few of sexuality. Even Marilyn Monroes shrivel and die. You, Mona, will die someday."

Mona's eyes had trouble blinking. To blink would be to miss a millisecond of Nero's white teeth as he spoke. "I will die some day," said Mona. The bare statement inflated her crotch. For the first time in her life she found the thought of her death arousing. She imagined a lifetime of excess and indulgence taxing and fattening and stressing her body until death would come as a relief to the frame and organs and brain and old, overused tongue. *I will die someday.* Nero wrapped around her like a boa. *Someday my body will turn blue, bloat, stink, decay,* Mona thought. *But now I am powerful, a goddess compared to the corpse I'll be after death.* Mona's heart pounded like police at a door.

Nero grinned proudly, flaunting his white teeth. "The world is at your tongue tip, Mona," Nero whispered. " There's no time to worry about limits. Your body craves all it can experience every moment. It knows the clock; it knows mortality. It's desperate and greedy. To hell with heaven and the Pearly Gates. You're heaven; I'm heaven. And sometimes we can be naughty. We can dabble in hell, too."

*This man's mouth is the Pearly Gates, those teeth that rip and chew meat. They could bite me awake. Chew me like meat.* Mona grasped for control. "But what's the use of it all if we die anyway?" she asked. The *Moonlight Sonata* seemed a figment from prehistory, a vague noise from a worthless, brutal past. *It's all the same stuff, all meat, all electric meat that's attracted to other electric meat.*

The beautiful man pointed a finger and touched it to her nose. "Fun, Mona. For fun. Come into the bedroom with me, Mona."

Mona could only nod. They drifted into the bedroom.

"How old are you, Mona?" Nero asked, unbuttoning her blouse.

"I'm...uhh...I'm thirty..."

Mona's shirt blew apart. "Have you been with many men?"

"No..."

The man nestled his nose behind her ear. Mona couldn't feel his large hands. She imagined them circling her body like warplanes, choosing their targets, preparing to attack erogenous territory. She pretended to be a blindfolded prisoner before a firing line, waiting for the teasingly delayed bullets. Mona waited for Nero's absent hands as he swabbed her ear with the sly muscle in his mouth. Soon his hands would meet her flesh like hammers. She felt her

67

shirt glide down her legs and over her feet. Mona's bowels tightened; her neck went limp.

"Only...a few...men," she admitted. Knowing she was crashing, Mona tried to stabilize. She tried to focus on the gloomy, sober first movement of the *Moonlight*, but her body was all Presto Agitato.

"They were lucky men, weren't they, Mona?" Nero taunted. "Lucky to have touched you, to have experienced you. Their death-aware bodies were desperate gluttons for your body, your lucky body."

"Yes, yessss...lucky..." No Havens to save her now. She was alone against this devil.

"Why did you let them, Mona?" the man asked, unzipping the back of her skirt.

"Because they wanted me," said Mona. "They desired me." *It's happening. I've held out, but now it's happening. I'm letting it happen. Letting him, letting him...*

Nero's hands finally clenched around her. He lifted her arms above her head. Mona gasped. Nero ran a finger from her arms to her waist. "This is all there is. Life is short and bodies are shorter. The body is the sole meaning in the universe. Once it ends, you end. Once you end, another body takes your place. This body is all there is, Mona. Let me please it. Let me share its brief meaning."

"Okay...I'll let you..."

"The moon can watch. I'm the Big Bad Wolf, Mona. Don't worry about anything but the bright red now in your body..."

Mona let the man ravage her. Through the window the moon glared at them like a disapproving mother. She felt the backs of her legs strike the bed and fell back.

*We smell,* thought Mona, waking the next morning. *So much for glorious bodies. We smell.* Nero lay on his back, snoring. His mouth gaped. Mona could slightly see his eyeballs between the eyelids. He looked dead. His nipples were hard in the morning cold. They were pale and weird. Every mole on his belly and chest repulsed her now. She could smell his sour breath.

"We're decaying everyday," Havens had often said. "We're in a constant struggle against degradation and rot." Mona hadn't allowed herself to think of Havens since she first visited Nero's penthouse. She could hardly remember Havens' face as she lay on the smelly bed. She not only smelled Nero, but she smelled herself on Nero. And Nero on her own body. *Never again,* she thought. *Never, never again. What was I thinking? How did he get here? I don't even know his last name! I know how he sounds in ecstasy but not his full name!*

The rude sun filled the room, boasting the same light that had illuminated the moon last night. Mona once liked the sun. Lately she dreaded it. It made her feel tired, exposed, and ugly. She felt so much prettier at night.

Mona studied Nero's vulnerable body. She could hack it to chunks with an axe if she wanted. She found it difficult to believe it had so pleased her only hours ago. How quick, the body's fall from grace. She turned away.

"Good morning, legs." A hand touched her bare back.

"Good morning," Mona said, standing. The hand touched her butt.

"Yummy," said Nero.

Mona retrieved her panties and slipped into them. "I need a shower."

"Oh? I thought we could go for Round Three."

*Twice. The first time I let him and we did it twice. I'm already used! Used!* "I'm sore. Sorry."

"Ah, the pain of pleasure."

Mona turned and suddenly asked, "How many women have you done this with, Nero?"

"How many women? Why?"

"Why? Because we had sexual intercourse all night, that's why! I want to know what kind of man I'm really with!"

Nero shook his head like a toying parent with a child. "Got things backwards, don't you, Mona? Why does it matter now?"

"It doesn't," Mona snapped, getting a towel

from the hall closet.

"Want me to make us breakfast?" Nero called.

"I'm not hungry!" She slammed the bathroom door.

Once the hot water struck her skin she began to feel better. She lathered soap over her body, scrubbing as if shedding shame and regret. Havens, Mona thought, *I'll never forget the waterfall. How it veiled us from the others, though we could see them, like a two-way mirror.* The thought of Havens invigorated the cleansing.

Mona closed her eyes and concentrated on the steam and the water's strong pressure. "Washing the animal away is a sacred activity," Havens always said. "Civilization is so fragile, so easily degraded." Mona decided that she'd break it all off with Nero as soon as she finished her shower. *Never again, never again,* she vowed.

Mona believed so even when she saw Nero's form through the translucent shower curtain and steam. She believed so even when the shower curtain opened on one side and Nero stepped in. She believed so even when Nero's hands ran through the lathered soap on her body. But when his mouth began to work its black magic, Mona lost her belief in soap. Mockery rained on her; all her noble will wilted. *Not like Havens. Nothing like him,* she thought. *Not like Havens. Nothing like Havens.*

*Worshipping nothing more than my body. Not me,*
*just my body. Not like Havens. Nothing like him.*
*And I love it. I love it. I love it, love it, love it…*
Mona spilled to her knees and returned the
worship in a wet blindness.

# In the Hands of a Living God

Jesus went digital in 1972 with the watches—
corner of Bourbon & Iberville Jesus' agent stares
into a sea of sin, pile of tracts sodden & limp at
his feet, glowing red in the word of god as it
flashes in red dots the length of the crossbeam
of the cross Jesus' agent holds up with one
uncertain hand, a paper trail to Calvary. Follow
the tracts, look in the gutters where they lay
scuttled & coated with a viscous film of spittle,
beer, vomit, the grey slush of shoe trackings
smeared in clumsy lines across the words,
"Love not the world, neither the things that are
in the world. If any man love the world, the love
of the father is not in him. For all that is in the
world, the lust of the flesh, and the lust of the
eyes, and the pride of life, is not of the father,
but is of the world. And the world passeth
away, and the lust thereof: but he that doeth the
will of God abideth forever."
Jesus went digital, the word of our lord
flashing by blurring by in luminous red dots &
too verbose for the crowd on Bourbon Street, an
endless animal stream each drop bent in deadly
intensity on the lust of the flesh and the pride of
life…& Oh! It is a fearful thing to fall into the
hands of the living god, make that double when
one happens to be stone drunk at the moment of
arrival—Jesus went digital when? Today,
around 7:30 when the agent of Christ drug the
cross (supplied, unlike the original, with a

small, detachable rubber wheel) out the front door of the Happy Christian Home for Wayward Souls to the corner of Bourbon & Iberville, though popular suspicion has it the transition took place much earlier, nearer the arrival of the first LCD watches, & before that was neon and the first neon cross, "I am the way and the light..."

Tonight it's a red light, Bourbon Street ambiance catching at the frayed edges of the robe of the living god & the meek looking creature who would take up his word, swallowing hard at the pressing crowd armed with beer cans & leers & in no mood at all to haggle. This sea, this street, Bourbon Street, is no place for a local, & that includes this man, a rather frightened looking young man holding up a cross & trying to hand out small booklets to passers-by, to be read once more sober, the man & the cross awash in demonic red, as if standing at the gates of hell itself. The man twists his sweating head pavement-wards as two young black kids no more than twelve — it well past midnight on Bourbon Street — nudge the agent of Christ's elbow with not the barest pretence of avoiding him, jarring the out-crooked elbow of the agent of Christ & thereby spill a good three dozen tracts, spraying from this timid fellow's fumbling hands out onto piss-slick street aflutter with red red red & fast receeding laughs of street punks. Reaching for the papers, the digital cross sways perilously in the supporting hand, so that for a moment it looks like the surest bet on Bourbon Street that tonight Jesus' red light will be extinguished, until the man from the Happy Christian Home for Wayward Souls remembers, at the last possible instant, the cross, catches it & shifts his gaze uncertainly from the seemingly endless stream of humans swarming, to the gutters, to the fluorescent haze of shops, back to the tracts at his feet.

From all directions the unmistakeable and all permeating smell of alcohol: this is my blood, this is this riot, this is the sloppy grin of the too well-off, too fat, too ridiculous in middle age woman dripping over a second story balcony dangling a string of beads over the wrought iron like bait, mouth a twisted, inelegant cavity of blood red above her faux satin dress, "Show your cock!" In another minute the beads drop to dim grasping hands below, faux satin woman leaning over the wrought iron deliriously, spilling her drink, too far gone to remember any of this, breasts threatening to tumble from the low scoop of her dress. The sheen of her dress is brown, shimmers in neon everywhere the brown shimmer the pink & garish red, the yellow of neons blaring off her dress an obscenity of haircurlers and lapdogs, the too dread this woman is flashing in the color of her dress, "Show your cock!" Somewhere she's found more beads, more bait, more beer. In Iowa next week she'll be telling her friends about St. Louis cathedral over coffee, but tonight, tonight she belongs to anyone who will have her. Somewhere two stories below, lost in the moil of Bourbon Street, the man who brought her here, the man who watches television in her home & answers to the name of *husband*, is by no means to be found bathed in the red pool of light cast by the word of our living god, "Show your cock!" Fury welling up, there, her face alight in it, with the question of why it is she wants tonight to scream this, why she needs to drink so much to scream this, fury choked down hard with a vicious upturn of the glass in her hand & whirl back into the room for more beer, more beads, more.

This is my blood the luminous blood of red dots...in the stone doorway, in the space where brick meets crumbling wood the sounds of the street coalesce, shivers through lingerers, jazz standards, bass of blues, gospel leaks out onto Bourbon Street. In the gaps of walls huddled in a ludicrous attempt to corral this roil, bricks straining lunacy leaking through the cracks. In dim cubbyholes black kids stamp their sneakers down hard on upturned bottlecaps, the teeth biting into the rubber of their shoes forming

make-shift taps for dancing, dancing next to
shallow cardboard boxes, following no rhythm
more complex than hunger. Tourists toss them
quarters out of no sentiment more noble than
guilt, women cooing at their dates "Isn't he
cute?" & the roll of a twelve-year-old's eyes on
Bourbon Street past midnight surrounded by
too too familiar sounds.

This is my body, this is the spill of Bourbon
Street, this is the smear of humanity through 2
A.M. when the last stragglers wobble
deliriously home certain this week's tourists
want nothing more at this delicate hour than to
hear the song, the phrase, the rant that glows
red in the wash of thousands like them turned
loose into the things of the world. Salvation of
neon. Promised land of titty bars. The happy
drinking grounds at last, oh, take me drunk! To
the hands of the living god whose blood is wine
& flesh bread to sop the morning's acid up
with. Here the lights never go out, blinding the
white of cheap t-shirts, palms, tarot read here,
& "On the inside!", just past the door with no
key, just past the man with the truncheon, just
past everything you can't quite get past lies the
land where all of this flows eternally & without
pain, where every drink is on the house &
everything you've ever desired shall be
delivered, "On the inside!" — the price of
salvation, the afterthought of doormen, the

patter and wiggle of wet fingertips pointing the
way through this doorway, through these gates,
through to the living god.

# I Dream of Bicycles

I dream of bicycles, of riding bicycles a
hundred feet high. I'm never conscious of the
absurdity, I'm just riding, pedaling from a great
height, looking down on the intersections I'm
passing through, the cars I fearfully somehow
manage to avoid. I strain and wobble, knowing
a crash or fall could happen any time. I
negotiate a turn, a traffic jam, I avoid a pile-up.
I hop onto an overpass, wrenching the towering
machine up to the eight lanes of perpendicular
concrete, then letting it drop back down while
somehow staying upright, aloft, somehow
continuing on my journey to I don't know
where, I never know where.

# Life Amongst the Ashes

She counted the money in her purse for the fifth time that morning and wondered what she was going to do. Rising from the chipped linoleum table, she crossed the kitchen and headed down the hallway to the closet. The door hung open, hinting at the blackness beyond, the emptiness. For one brief, horrific moment, she felt the same. She saw that blackness, that emptiness as the escape from her daily meal of fear and concern.

In the living room, she heard her children talking as they watched the television and replaced the blackness with longing, sadness and relief. She had no time for this, no time to wallow in empty desires of an easy way out. She had no choice, and that was the real soul killer. She had to accept and go on even though each step hurt so much.

Some days it felt as if every step she took ripped a little piece of her off. A slice of skin here, a bit of flesh there. She felt all bones and rags as she maintained a brave, stoic facade on the crumbling building of her life. Quietly and pretending as if she were rearranging things, she searched the pockets of all the coats. All the shabby and outdated coats. Coats that had not been that nice when purchased but had at least been affordable.

Frayed cuffs and tears in pockets were the least of the problems that marred this fashion show. There were stains and burns, catches and tears that could not be hidden or mended. Each one was its own pothole, its own empty storefront of a dying city. Once the shabbiness set in, it was almost impossible to escape.

She ran her hands through the pockets, down past the holes and deep into the liners. Maybe she had missed something. Maybe, somehow, that one thing that she so desperately needed would be there. Today her daughter had a school outing - nothing fancy, nothing really great, but still it had a price. Five dollars, an insignificant amount, but an amount she didn't have to spare.

Years ago, when the fat of life had started to slip, she learned the necessity of trimming. She cut corners here, made do there, sacrificed everything to try to maintain just the status quo, just to remain even. But that never works. Slowly, the shabbiness started to appear, the wearing down, the breaking, the worn through. Inch by inch the level, low as it was, started to descend even further.

One unexpected bill, one surprise cost and everything was thrown into disarray. It didn't take much, it wasn't fortunes that made the difference but something as simple as five dollars. The entire class would be going, all the smiling faces as they escaped the drudgery of school for a diversion however limited. But her daughter could not go, would not be allowed to go without the precious and insignificant five dollars.

What could she do, she wondered as she stroked the coats absentmindedly. Could she call the school and beg for assistance, a week's delay in the need for the money? She would be able to get it somehow; ask a friend, call her parents even though she didn't dare, couldn't ask for more from those who had already given so much.

Maybe she could explain it to her daughter, tell her how she had nothing to give, nothing to offer to send her on the trip - but at what cost? The chance of the diversion... God how she wanted one herself, anything to let her out of her prison. She longed to run, to fly, to explore and laugh but she hadn't felt a real laugh in years and smiling almost hurt.

She had been through these coats before. Her hands had searched the pockets earlier in her desperation to find that one thing she needed. Even a little change would be a start. A few quarters here, a few dimes here and slowly she might scrape it together. If only she had a little more warning, an extra month to plan, to get ready for this, but she hadn't. The school had sent the note home Monday for a Wednesday departure and twenty-four hours just wasn't enough time.

Dejected, she stepped back from the closet and walked to her room. She dropped heavily onto the bed. Across from her, she saw her reflection in the mirror and suddenly wanted to scream. That was not her; that was not that beautiful and vibrant girl she had once seen there in the silvered glass. What she gazed at now was the face of a haggard woman, too thin and too worried, the lines of fear etching themselves into brittle and translucent skin.

She felt the tears well up inside her like some great geyser about to explode. She felt darkness creep in again, its tendrils black and oily at the periphery of her vision. All she wanted to do was succumb to it.

She wanted that darkness... To sleep, to escape this, to leave all these worries and weights behind. It could only be better, it could only be quieter in the grave. At least there, she would not hear the voices of doubt and denial that sang in her head.

She fought this battle daily, this battle between living and dying, between wanting to live and wanting to die. She thought of her children crying, she could see them weeping at her gravesite and wondering why she had chosen to do what she had done. Some days that was enough to break her of her deserved self-pity. Other days it almost fortified her resolve. She would be dead, she would hear no cries, see no tears. She would be free.

She wondered at them, those children who lived totally unaware of her agonies. She did her best to try and maintain the appearances for her daughter. It was so much more difficult being a girl. Appearances were everything, clothes and shoes defined not only who you were but the friends you could have.

Show up badly dressed, and for your sufferings you could expect more. You would be ostracized, ignored, taunted, marked for life. No matter what happened, what changes of fortune occurred, you would always remember how badly you felt that day. Women lived their entire lives scarred by the happenings on playgrounds and classrooms. A cruel word, a mean gesture, a single taunt could lead to tears, embarrassment and the horror of ever returning again.

The girls, the other ones, those angels. They would descend like hawks amongst doves to devour those that didn't fit the mold. Later, regardless of anything else, that one victim would be forever watched, forever preyed upon. In so many ways it was so much easier to raise a boy.

She steadied herself on the bed, seeing in her mind's eye what her children would most likely be doing right now. Her daughter would be in the bathroom curling her hair and primping for the day's appearances. Her meager collection of clothes would be accented, switched, mixed and matched to belie the limited numbers. Add a belt here, a scarf there, maybe something bright to distract the eye, the daughter was already skilled in hiding.

She saw the hungry look in her daughter's eyes as they passed clothing stores. She could almost smell the desire to at least try on the beautiful things, but she had learned. To go into the shop would only lead to the overwhelming, searing need to possess. Possession was out of the question. Any more than a passing glance would lead her to her own sorrow.

This was the life of want, the life of need that that slowly broke away little pieces until finally she felt like crumbling. It was a life of disappointment and hidden secret tears. While she could understand her daughter's response to the situation, she could not understand her son's. The son seemed to live in an easy oblivion to everything.

If he had books to read or quiet private games to play then he was happy. A cardboard box was a spaceship for days, sheets of paper became the controls of a destroyer once penciled in. She wondered at his oblivion, wishing she could experience the same.

He had learned the secret early on and he maintained it well. He had learned that by not caring, he never felt the pain. By not really paying attention, he was free of the concerns and minutia that plagued everyone else. He learned that disappointment was so all consuming that he could either ignore it or die by it.

His friends' toys were cooler and more varied. Their houses were bigger and more spacious. Their lives were fuller and greater in the promise they held. If he really paid any attention, he would fall to the ground and never ever get up.

The woman sat on the edge of the bed, her world an empty shell of grey pain and disappointment. The mirror across from her was her enemy and she wanted to smash it, to throw something through it, but she knew she couldn't. For all that it was, it was still furniture and that was something they could ill-afford to replace. The mirror, for all its faults, was still too useful, too needed to be discarded so easily.

She was just about to walk back out to the living room and her daughter's disappointment when she spotted it. Folded like a tiny little Japanese kimono and tucked into the plastic grip around the mirror was something she could not believe. Tentatively, she approached the object. She wanted to run out of the room, ignore it, pretend she hadn't seen it. It was a lot easier to ignore it, if she did, it couldn't let her down, it couldn't shatter her hopes.

But she couldn't give up, not now, not with her arm stretching towards the silly, folded shape. With shaking hands, she reached out and plucked it from the frame where it had stayed for years, forgotten, unnoticed. As she held it, she remembered what it was and a flood of memories came back to her.

There had been happier times when they were still a family, when everything and anything seemed possible. They had been sitting around the kitchen table one night when the son wanted to show off his latest skill. He had done some origami in art class and now anything that could be folded was being folded. He took a bill from his father and quickly creased it into the tiny shape she saw before her now. The father had laughed that it was expensive doll's clothing but he had never unfolded it. It had, instead, been tucked into the frame and here it still sat.

Sentimentality was the first to go when need rose its ugly head. With her heart beating solidly in her chest, she unfolded the dusty doll and sat in stupefied amazement at what she held. A five-dollar bill made up the kimono; a ten made the doll inside and another five was folded into the belt. She was holding a fortune, or at least a fortune to her.

For a lot of the people who would be passing

by her apartment that morning, twenty dollars was chump change. They might blow that on some pointless purchase or a good lunch. To them, the twenty would mean little or nothing in their scheme of things. To her, however, it meant more than she would even be able to tell. That simple amount meant freedom. For a few days she would be free of the immediate fear. For a little while, she would feel good about things and have some faith in how they might turn out.

# This is Not a Psychotic Love Poem

I won't mention
that I've counted
the hairs on the back
of your neck thirty-two
times in the last
four minutes.

I won't point out
that I sleep with a grocery
list you once threw away.

I won't imply
that I lurk outside
your window every night
just to watch you read.

I won't suggest
that when I close
my eyes I see your mouth.

I won't insinuate
that your hair
smells like laundry
and patchouli mixed
with a touch of chlorine,
and is as soft
as the underside
of orchid petals.

# Have You Seen America?

Not the sprawling growth
television Los Angeles grey
plastic icons, six for a dollar
whitest smile, the perfect 10
oozing parking lot pools
streetlight-washed nights.

Not the tourist-ridden apple
bargain mementos of T-shirt sentiment
coursing rows between stacked piles
flat-faced canyons lined
with dingy yellow taxi-cab ornaments
in ribbons of gasping congestion.

No.
I mean America.
The expanse of destiny.
The interior fertile heartlands.
The millions of square miles
untapped, untold, in between.

Cherry phosphate, cheeseburger
for here or to go?
road-side paradise in your car
shotgun blasted rusty Stop sign
hold the pedal down
through America.

Dirt road, low-water bridge
cornfield, tractor truck

mountain bluff forested
bullfrog singing through swamp fog
snow caps in the desert
take a picture of America.

Sleeping beneath the stars
crescent moon throws a shadow
deer, coyote, buffalo
skunks, bear and possum
share what we've named
America.

Blizzard, tornado
squall, lightning
Dust-storm scrubbing
rolling tumbleweeds
by the barbed wire fences
of America.

Motorcycle sleeping bag,
bandana and black leather boots,
mirrored sunglasses,
lizard and scorpion tattoo,
greasy, sleeveless shirt
on the back of America.

Guitar ballad on a river,
summertime, porch side blues,
dirty night-club hybrid mix,
garage-band rock and roll,

radio-dancing, re-invention of the soul
of America.

Speak your mind.
Gather in the streets.
Due process and equality.
Worship in peace. Bear arms!
Congress shall make no law
in America.

Taxes, elections, community
and listen up!
Freedom isn't free.
Obligation to do
not only complain.
Pay your dues to America.

Bring us yours to our shores,
melting another, cultural infusion
making new history together,
lose yourself to find it again,
the second chance
of America.

Walk your dog in the evening.
Drink a beer with your neighbor.
See the flag the waves for you
watch the kids play into dusk
and see the new
America.

Get OUT of the port!
The city and hotel is only a glimpse.
Sail into the deeper waters.
Get lost for days.
Have you seen
America?

# The Distraction

There was something comforting in his garage, something honest and sincere.

He turned on the light; the first switch was rigged to the work bench, the second switch to the overhead, and the third was for both. He even installed a dimmer switch. It was during the *Time Life* books phase of his life. He got a new book each month with details on how to do a different aspect of home improvement. Electrical was amazing; easy and complicated at the same time, dangerous and thrilling when it was finished right. He liked the electrical stuff. That was, '87, '88, a long time before cable tv made working on your home a source of entertainment. He kind of resented the television lately, he kind of resented the fact that the American flag and National Anthem doesn't play and the television never signs off. It was unnatural in a way. He remembered coming home from 'Nam, and waiting to see the test pattern. It was one of those things he imagined before he went to sleep overseas, one of the images he longed for, knowing that when he saw it he would be home.

The world was different from the moment he got on the plane; his life was cut and pasted and shredded, all because of that one ride on a plane. He spent the remainder of his life trying to forget those three years. Somehow, when he least expected it, a shadow of those days would

sneak into his mind, sneak into the California
sunsets, and women he was attracted to, and
early mornings when he surfed before anyone
else in the world was awake. The jungle: The
rapid pulse of automatic weapons rattling
overhead, days knee deep in mud and nowhere
to sleep, flies and mosquitoes, daily death, the
heat, the orange moon. It would all sneak into
the mind and cast its shadow, interrupt his life.

Claim his life, it wasn't fair, he didn't relive
the first years of his marriage to that beautiful
sweetheart with the curly red hair and beautiful
skin; those memories of touching and laughing
never snuck in his mind like that. The memories
of his dad and mom and visits to the Italian
coast, they didn't pervade his mind; in fact he
had to force the memories that were good,
because they were fading, fading and blending
and losing their power.

But not the three years, no, not Hell. Hell
only gains power; it keeps you from loving,
making commitments, keeps you from enjoying
your children's birthdays because right there in
the back yard you start to weep like a woman,
knowing your friend Jimmy would never see
his kid and remembering him passing you the
picture of his wife and baby in the pouring rain.
Precious cargo, that picture. Remembering
taking it off, with body in flight and leaving him
there empty-eyed, and running with his picture

in hand and not thinking that... that "minute" in your life would never leave you and make you resent your own kids and "why him and not me," and you have to go for a long drive that your wife doesn't understand and fight about it later, because you can't explain what is the matter.

You spend years trying not to think about the days when you were 19 and you couldn't sleep and had to walk and walk and walk, and started to see things because you were so tired, and those sleepless ghouls, those demons in the trees under moonlight...they never leave. They crop up 'round blind corners of grocery stores, and late nights leaving bars and in between women's legs when you're going down...but you want to forget and you get limp because those images prevent you from living and the bitch gets angry and you can't focus because you're haunted and no one gets your silence. You're fleeing your non-response at times, "Is not about them. It's not about them at all, it's not even about you. It's about those fucking three years in Hell, it's about your mind's power, your memory's power, the snapshot, video camera in your brain."

He loved his garage, his Craftsman tools, his American made Craftsman tools, always steel, made to last forever, made to do the job right. His miter saw, jig saw, planer, dremmel, band

width, hand sanders, finish sander, palm, rack
and racks of shellac, stain, wood dye, rust
remover, strippers, shelves of sandpaper, 50
grit, 100 grit, 150.

The sawdust curled in tiny pieces sitting on
the counter. The smell of paint, varnish, wood
and solvents, and the wall of tools, each piece of
steel that willed to life, tables, chairs, shelves,
handles, and ornate music boxes for nieces, and
daughters and grand daughters.

Here he could sit on his chair and listen to
Mozart or Miles Davis and think about the
wood's grain, and angle of the cut, and plane
the edges. Here the sound of the saw rising
above the violins, or base, or voice on the
recorder gave him so many things to focus on
he could not be found. His mind would be
harnessed, aware of each second and not aware
of any moments, the task at hand made him
part of the life of the immediate.

His hair was white now. He kept busy. He
was thinking about that girl he met with the
dark eyes that laughed too much and told him
she wanted to die when she was sixty, and sixty
wasn't far off from him, just a couple of years
and it made him want to reach over and slap
her cocky face. She didn't know what that
meant. To die. She went on and on telling him
how she was so mad at this one person that she
could kill them. She had no idea. She had not

seen death in all its fury, in all its random whims, come and take, like a savage beast. He no longer wanted to have anything to do with her. He just wanted to get away from this flippant disrespect for life. He thought about how women could be so self-centered, and callous, the gentler sex? Right?

As he walked to his work bench he thought about her laugh, and how silly females could be and how she was too old to act like that, and how much her dark skin made him want to touch it. And how he hated her now.

And why he kept running.

Why couldn't he just tell her, tell her that she made him angry?

Why couldn't he tell anyone what he wanted, or didn't want, and why was his mouth permanently fused closed when things mattered. Why? Because no one gets it, no one.

And he turned on his tape and let Mozart began his evening. He sat at his bench and pulled out a piece of wood, and looked at the drawing – and got comfort in the distraction.

## The Bus

When you're standing at a bus stop
Just past midnight,
All you ever really know is the safety of your
surroundings,
The stillness of your own shadow
While staring at the shape of smoke
That may as well be breath
In this thumb numbing Southwestern
sweatshirt weather Winter.
So like a scumbag scarecrow standing stoic
somewhere splintered
Between the reality of exact change
And the fantasy of cab fare,
I choose to chain away a fraction of my day's wages
While I play with the split ends of my exaggerated
facial hair,
Admiring how this skinny Indy kid
Crying inside my Discman
Has learned to market his wear and tear
And the fact that I spent my last dime
To support his dream
Makes me that much more aware of how
squandered my days have been.
Each day I wake
To work the window shoppers to stop on a whim
And spark their customized electronic strips
While pretending not to notice how
The surly service worker's clothes and life
Look slept in
Or

99

How from the elevated windows of their
weekend war machines
I'm just another set of antennae in a cluster of
Anonymous public transit headphone drones
On our way home to somewhere we've had to learn
To adjust our hurry to get to...
...but I'm not about preaching poverty to you people.
I'm just a tourist to transport transience.
I wasn't bred like these chickens in 12" compartments
To compliment a side of Ranch.
I was spun 'round with high hopes
On a shiny rotisseries,
Carefully stuffed with citrus
And left to go bad.
Bad like that bad middle class habit of leaving
Shit like kids unfinished when something better
could be bought
But
These are just my Jacks,
Faking like their Aces
While smirking behind my reticent pedestrian
poker face
As I situate my window seat and great
My actor for the stage.
Enter: The creepy late-night white guy,
Sporting pit stains and smoke stench
Like some sample platter of first world putrefaction
And I assure you
You don't want any part of this mess.
Why don't you go sit next to the sleeping old man

With the colostomy bag showing
Or the overweight black woman
Cussing and ripping her weave to shit
To scratch at mats of dandruff
Or even the fatigued transvestite
Complete with slip lip and single dangling handcuff.
Take your pick from this whole cavalcade for a
baby face
Once used to instill trust in a murder victim...
Fear
And anything else we have to tell ourselves
To justify this shared six inches of silence
Is best left unsaid
As you turn your book into a barricade
To shield a face full of dread
I'll pretend not to notice pages
Pretending to be read.
Instead
I'll shove my mind through this window
With thoughts that move three stops a minute
And look between the hard dark eyes of tonight
Into the light that tomorrow begins with
Where death scenarios grow silent
With the coming of the dawn
Because on survival island
Life is a stop requested
And unnecessary conversation is prohibited
By law.

## Sonnet of a Godmother

Vodka tastes a bit like battery acid on its own,
but you add amaretto to it, and it opens up
like a flowering wound, or a young girl looking
for love.
She cradles the glass while it condenses in her
bones,
sucks it down quickly, and again.
Her cheeks flush and she's red enough
for comradery as she bellies up, plays tough
at the bars in Hollywood, challenges men
to dart games under the pale red lights,
pulls them into the bathroom stalls
for quick fixes of adrenaline,
as they pull up her skirt, she eases her fight
for it's just another night after all
and some things are worse than consumption.

# That's the Way Love Goes

### The Meeting

They roll passionately on the bedroom floor.
They are both lost in the rapture of the moment,
in the act at hand. Neither can believe this is
happening; but it is, without a doubt,
happening. It is, in a word, wonderful, and
more glorious than any dream.

Las Vegas can be an exciting place especially
to those who have never danced cheek-to-cheek
with its dark lustful soul. It is many things to
many people for many reasons; to some it is a
Technicolor playground filled with endless
neon-bathed wonder and to others a relentless
raging inferno of forbidden temptation and
despair. To him, it is just a weekend away from
the normal tortures of life in Barstow,
California. One month ago he and an old buddy
had decided to meet there and like everything
else in his life, all had gone according to plan. It
had been a long time since he and his old high
school pal had seen each other, seven years to
be exact. Yes, everything had gone according to
plan, almost.

As she leaves the casino after another long
hard shift of dealing cards, she thinks to herself,
"Tonight is the last night I'm working here." She
hates working in casinos most of which are
located in the gross bellies of nightmarishly
egocentric architectural monstrosities whose

outrageous room rates she could never hope to afford. She has come to loathe the seemingly endless wave of tourists who crash down over the Strip every single night; she hates their inflated egos, their low-budget tips, their disgusting backroom habits and humor, and most of all their puerile ability to blame her when they lose all their money at the table. She is a card dealer and although she thought she had prepared herself for the realities of living in the largest money-driven entertainment Mecca in the world, she had not, it seemed, prepared herself well enough.

It had been one year ago almost to the day that she had stepped off the Greyhound bus in Las Vegas, Nevada. It had been a long journey from Madisonville, Kentucky but she had made it. As she steps onto the escalator leading down to the south side exit she remembers her almost uncontrollable exhilaration at seeing, for the first time, what seemed like an endless carnival of lights that is, for better or worse, Las Vegas. For her, a wide-eyed Midwestern girl, it had been a once in a lifetime moment. That had been one year ago and now, as BB King soulfully wails in his legendary blues song, "The thrill is gone."

Now she is a dealer in a casino and now, once again, she hates her life. It's two am, Friday morning when she walks through the revolving door exit of the hotel. As the warm desert wind kisses her sad and tired face she thinks, "It's going to be a boring weekend."

No one in Las Vegas noticed when on a warm Saturday evening at approximately seven pm a rather plain-featured young woman walking briskly down Flamingo Boulevard, not paying attention to anything in particular, bumped into two casually dressed well-groomed young men, apparently in deep discussion, walking in the opposite direction. No one in Las Vegas noticed when one of the young men instinctively reached out and touched her on the shoulder to keep her from stumbling. No one could tell that both of their hearts skipped a beat when their bodies made contact for the first time; certainly not the young man's companion.

They, however, noticed; the man and woman who met each other on that beautiful wonderful warm sweet Saturday Vegas evening. They would talk about it for many, many years to come for you see, "That's The Way Love Goes."

## Summa Summarum

the sum of sums
is that we can never give
more than we take

that autumn will tumble into spring
without winter being noticed

loneliness becomes a need to escape the crowds

and even the brightest of sunrises
inevitably turns into falling sunsets
holding on with its burgeoning embers

(previous published in *Adagio Verse Quarterly*)

# The Boy With the Fire in His Eyes and the Girl who Loved Him
## (a contemporary fairy tale)

When Sorjuana Cadiz met Xavier Bardao on a warm August night in Barcelona, she remembered how his eyes were so dark that they acted like mirrors, which reflected the candlelight at a café table on Las Ramblas so brilliantly that they seemed to be forged of living fire. When she told Xavier this, he only smiled and told her that she should be careful of what she said, and so she became quiet and stared into his eyes that echoed each flicker and dance of the candles.

Exactly twelve months and three days later, Xavier proposed to Sorjuana, saying that he loved her with all his soul. He got down on one knee in broad daylight at 14:42 at the entrance of the grand unfinished Gaudí cathedral known as Sagrada Familia on August 17th. It was a Thursday, and it was hot. Three tourist buses had disgorged their minions, who took snapshots of the strikingly handsome Spanish boy proposing to the most exquisitely beautiful Spanish girl on the steps just below the entrance, where a Cubistic Christ, attended by his weeping apostles, looked down in pain from his stone cross.

"I knew I shouldn't have let you propose to me on such a hot day as that," Sorjuana would

107

later say. For, that August 17th day was the hottest day in Barcelona in 97 years. It was strangely dry also, which was unusual for this city that danced right next to a clear blue Mediterranean Sea. In fact, it was so dry and so hot that the air seemed to be made of little particles of white fire. This phenomenon, scientists said two days later, was the result of a heavy saturation of salt crystals in the air which the Mediterranean Sea had let loose from her skirt after her heated dance with the sun.

"How was I to know it would be so hot?" laughed Xavier. "I would have proposed to you on that day even if it had snowed and the statues wore beards of ice," and he kissed her full red lips and ran his fingers through her dark hair that always seemed to him to smell faintly of fresh oranges as if she had just come in from the Andalusian citrus groves in the south of Spain.

"It never snows in Barcelona," replied Sorjuana, and she did not mention that at the moment Xavier had said, "I love you. Will you be my wife?" the sunlight ricocheted off a pane of stained glass, mingled with the brilliant white flashes in the air and set his eyes to such fearsome flames that it seemed he would burn up from the intensity of the fire. But, she remembered that the last time she had mentioned his eyes Xavier had told her not to remark about it. It was a bright morning, and his eyes blazed with the promise of a fierce sun, and she kissed him back, inhaling the minty traces of shaving cream on his face, a face which to her seemed to be a reincarnation of the noble faces of the old Spaniards from the days of the Romans.

Exactly two years and four months later, on Christmas Eve, Sorjuana gave birth to their first child. Their doctor had asked if they wanted to know the child's sex so they could name it ahead of time and be spared a hasty decision that the child might regret later in life, but they both said that they preferred the mystery. So, on December 24, at 20:17 PM, Sorjuana brought into this world a baby boy, and they named him Enric.

"He looks just like you, my love," said Sorjuana as the baby Enric closed his tiny fingers about a strand of her long hair and nestled down to sleep against her breast to hear once more the sound of his mother's heart.

"How does anyone know who a baby looks like?" replied Xavier. "He hasn't been in this world long enough for time to carve him a face like mine anyway," he said as he kissed Enric on the cheek and then kissed Sorjuana so tenderly that she could feel his heart beat into her own.

"Babies can have their father's eyes,"

Sorjuana said affectionately.

"He hasn't opened his yet," Xavier whispered, "He might have your eyes."

Xavier climbed in bed next to Sorjuana. It was raining hard, and the wind blew the water against the window in horizontal sheets. The weatherman would later say that Barcelona had not seen a storm of this magnitude in over one hundred years. Streets flooded, the ocean swept in through the marina and over the jetties, the sea gulls had flown in as far as Madrid, some seven hours away by fast train, and days later little children playing soccer in the streets far from the sea would find a piece of seaweed or even a fish still swimming in a pool of salty water. Xavier pulled the blanket up to Sorjuana's neck and put his arm around her and Enric. It was wonderful to hear a strong storm outside. In his mind Xavier believed that a winter child would be a strong child, and as the rain poured and the wind grew ever stronger, he felt that the universe was pumping its own primal energy into their baby boy.

"Yes," smiled Sorjuana, "Enric will be just like you, sweetheart."

Exactly seven days later, Enric opened his eyes. Sorjuana and Xavier had brought him into the doctor because it seemed strange that a baby's eyes should stay shut for so long.

"Maybe he wants the privacy of his dreams a

little longer," said Xavier, not really all that worried about the boy.

"Maybe," said Sorjuana, "there is something wrong and the longer we wait the worse it will be for him." It was night time when they brought Enric into the doctor's office, and Enric was fast asleep in his basket. The doctor first listened to his heart.

"His heartbeat's very strong," she said after listening to it for a count of one minute. "I'm afraid I'm going to have to wake him up to check his eyes," and she dimmed the lights and turned on a hand-held instrument that emitted a piercing light. Very carefully she focused the beam on Enric's little closed eyes. The skin was delicately colored, still the blush from nine months of his mother's womb. The light kindled the skin over Enric's eyes to beautiful orbs. Suddenly, the doctor let out a scream and the instrument fell from her hand. Xavier barely caught her as she fainted and almost struck her head against the hard floor.

The nurse, hearing the doctor's cry, rushed into the room and turned on the light.

"I knew he would have your eyes," Sorjuana said in amazement, and some fear.

"You never should have said they looked like fire when we first met," exclaimed Xavier as shocked and amazed as Sorjuana. The doctor said that Enric had opened his eyes when her

111

light shone on them. And there they were. Enric didn't have the eyes that anyone has. They were living flames, flickering, revolving, oranges and red swirling with sparks of white and blue. The fires did not leave his eye sockets. They stayed just as surely as others' eyes stay in their set boundaries. But they were flames nonetheless, and the doctor, after she recovered from the fright, said there was nothing she could do.

"We'd better keep him happy," said Xavier. "If he cries he might burn himself up."

So, Sorjuana and Xavier raised Enric as they would any other boy, except that they were certain that Enric never cried. And God seemed to be merciful, because never once did Enric ever show that he needed to cry. Enric went to school, had many friends, and he could see far better than anyone. He could look straight into the sun, and at night he could pierce the darkest of shadows. He was so handsome that when he grew into adulthood it seemed that even the statues turned to look at him, or that people turned into statues as they looked at him, so transfixed they were by his beauty. He excelled at soccer, and his scores at school were always the highest.

But one thing eluded him, and that was someone to love him. For, though he was as handsome as a Greek god and with his eyes of fire seemed as a god, no girl would give her heart to him. Enric seemed like he didn't belong to this world, and in their hearts they could not give their affections to a man with fire for eyes, no matter how handsome, smart and athletic he was, or kind. Enric was the perfect boy, the perfect son, the perfect friend. But in his perfection he became imperfect, especially for those of his own age.

Then one day he sat at the dinner table and didn't say a word to either his father or mother.

"What's wrong, Enric?" asked Sorjuana, although she and Xavier knew the answer. "You haven't said anything, and you haven't eaten at all."

"No one will love me," Enric said sadly. "If I were the type who could cry, I'd cry now."

"It takes a while for everyone to find someone to love them, Enric," reassured Xavier, "It will take a little longer for you." Enric's eyes died down to quiet blue flames. Only here and there a flash of red pierced the sadness.

Way up north in Sweden lived a very beautiful girl of twenty-one years, three months and seventeen days. Her name was Bibi Egeland, and although she was born and lived in Sweden, her parents were from Oslo, Norway. She was six feet tall, willowy, fair-skinned and had blonde hair that seemed as if it sprang from the Harvest Moon on a warm autumn midnight. She was the daughter of

113

Emilie Adrisson and Hjalmar Egeland, a couple who had fallen in love on December 24th, at 20:17 PM, at a Christmas Eve party for Norwegians working in Sweden. The news service said one week later that at 20:17 PM exactly, on December 24th, the temperature was the coldest ever recorded in Malmo, Sweden, which is where the couple ended up staying for the rest of their days.

In fact, all of Scandinavia was in a freeze when Bibi's parents met. It was so cold that the entire sea froze, so that people could actually skate from Sweden over to Denmark and have coffee with friends they usually only saw in the summer. It was so cold that the grey clouds turned blue and echoed the blue eyes of most of the people in those countries, but the color exactly matched Bibi's parents' eyes. It seemed as if the breath of Thor the Thunderer lived both in the air at that moment and in Emilie's and Hjalmar's eyes. Many people commented about the beautiful shade of blue that colored Emilie and Hjalmar's eyes exactly the same color. And everyone agreed that none had ever seen eyes the color of Emilie's and Hjalmar's.

Seventeen months and four days later the couple was married, and ten months after that Bibi was born. Bibi was a beautiful child, and her parents loved her deeply. The physician in Malmo, a geneticist in college, wanted to see if

114

the baby would have the exact shade of her eye color as her parents. He knew she had a twenty-five percent chance of inheriting their eye color, but something in his heart said that the laws of genetics and alleles, recessive and dominant, might change with this child. He was right. Bibi opened her eyes in his office one day later, but even he was unprepared for what he saw. For, instead of the delicate blue that seemed otherworldly and so exquisitely beautiful in her parents, little Bibi had the element of air for her eyes. They were light blue one moment, then the deep blue of midnight, or the grey of a cloudy day, and even at times they would swirl with blues, greens and greys so that it seemed a whirlwind danced in her sockets.

So Bibi grew up, a woman as beautiful as the Norse goddess Freyja, kind, intelligent, a wonderful skier and skater, a heart fond of laughter, yet she was alone. And Bibi didn't dare cry, for all of the doctors, the physicists, even the atmospheric scientists concurred that should Bibi cry she might unleash whirlwinds and tornadoes instead of tears.

The summer of Bibi's twenty-first year her parents decided to take her to a southern place where she could see beautiful sunsets over a warm and blue sea, hoping that she might forget for a while her beauty which although inspired wonderment, even reverence, failed to

115

inspire love.

It was August 10th in Cadaqués, a small village on the Mediterranean to the north of Barcelona, that the Egelands took a summer vacation house. It was an old fishing village frequented by artists, and it was on a small bay. The sunlight had the amazing quality of looking like it was shining through an immaculate and very thin piece of parchment made of the finest celestial materials. Bibi Egeland loved to walk around the north point to look beyond the bay. There was a small restaurant on the cliffs which served her favorite, a tapas that was an omelette with potatoes cooked inside. As it was always sunny, Bibi wore sunglasses to hide her eyes.

This particular August 10th day Bibi was finishing her *tapas* when she glimpsed a very handsome man sit down next to her. The man wore the same sunglasses as she, and he smiled, spoke in a rapid Catálan to a waiter and then looked over the sea. Bibi wondered about him. He seemed uncomfortable, as if his beauty was a flaw, or maybe he did not find himself as others saw him? Had she been able to see into his thoughts she would have known he was thinking the same about her. For Bibi also possessed a discomfort of someone who realizes she is flawed in some deep way forged by nature and not able to be fixed by humankind and so must be hidden both in countenance and in belief.

The waiter brought over a *tapas* of the fried potatoes known as *patatas bravas* to the man. Bibi tried them once and loved them, but *brava* means spicy in Spanish, and she found them delicious, yet too hot for her unaccustomed tongue. Still, she loved watching people eat them imagining what it would be like to be able to withstand the heat of the red sauce. At that moment a gust of wind blew in from the sea, a gust that seemed to be an arrow from the heart of the Mediterranean itself, comprised of air newly born and never breathed before this moment. The gust knocked the sunglasses from Bibi's face, and her eyes swirled a deep blue, and lightnings tap-danced around the edges and into the middles.

The man looked at her, at her eyes, and she quickly picked up her sunglasses and put them back on. But it was too late. The man walked over to her table and sat down. He asked her something in Spanish, then in Catálan, then in French. She could understand none of them, but she responded in Norwegian, Swedish, Danish and German. He shook his head. They stared at each other behind their dark sunglasses for so long it seemed the sun rose and set three times before the man moved.

Slowly he took off his sunglasses. And she

saw that instead of eyes he had living flames swirling in deep scarlet and orange hues. He slowly moved his hands to her sunglasses. He would have stopped if she wanted, but she didn't want him to stop. His eyes were so beautiful she wanted to see them without the mask of dark glass. She felt his fingers delicately wrap around her glasses; then he removed them, and he looked deep into her eyes. They were now the color of the air that clings to the surface of the Mediterranean Sea just as the morning breaks over the horizon.

"Enric," he said slowly. "Yo soy Enric."

"Bibi," she reponded.

They both stared into each others' eyes, watching each nuance, each subtle change. Behind them their parents approached and waved. But they stopped when they saw their children, their only children, looking into the eyes of the other.

Bibi placed her hands into Enric's waiting grasp. Enric felt her heart race, the slight traces of perspiration from anticipation, fear, the same feelings that rose up in him higher and higher until it seemed that the feelings were about to overflow. Enric stood up and walked Bibi to the edge of the cliffs high up over the sea.

Suddenly, he felt his eyes start to burn. He tried to hold back, but tears sprang forth and ran in living flames down his face. Bibi saw the

118

flames pour from Enric's eyes, and she suddenly felt the fiery cold taste of her own tears as they sped from her eyes. They held each other closely, each heartbeat quickening, matching the other, and still the tears came. Two whirlwinds sprang up at their feet. They were fed by the living fire that fell from Enric's eyes.

Soon the whirlwinds were rushing about them. Enric saw his tears become torrents of fire, but this was not a burning fire. It was a beautiful fire that nourished and fed. Higher and higher the winds rose until all that the shocked onlookers could see were two growing tornadoes of vivid flame. Suddenly, the two twisting vortices of fire leapt up into the sky. Together they danced across the Mediterranean Sea, at each touch leaving a splash of color, until they disappeared over the horizon outshining even the sunset.

## montana de oro

we are the girls with the cheesegrater hearts
wet red nicks inflicted with each involuntary
beat

with driveway spikes for teeth
piercing our lips
backing out every word uttered
with oedipal proportioned inevitability

we are the girls
with timebomb tongues
counting down until others
duck and cover
unable to contain the runaway train
of our freightweighted force of nature

with pocketfuls of shiny shards
with palmfuls of question marks
with bellyfuls of crackling chrysalis glittering

we are the girls
anointed in snake oil
we didn't covet

and now are we running
breathless
from screaming at joshua trees
in the rain
to make clean what was tainted
praying to be redeemed:

in/clemency

we are the girls exquisite in our comprehension
of excruciate
we spill love
we are leaking transmissions
from each duct

yet
for every breath we
ponder reversing

for every moment insurmountable

we are 10 fold beholden grateful
awestruck
at the vast and delicate delectation
of this particular and precious and tenuous
existence
we are bursting at the seams
innocent criminals
teeming with rubies

we make way

any helena will tell you
consider the orchid amputated and atrophying in
glass
note the skinned bloodball of discarded mink:
it is the nature of our species

to destroy what it desires
to consume
to violate and take
what it deems beauty

we make way

we are the girls trapped in concrete
only knowing there is a snowglobe inside
a memory floating in pale grace

a place where the bottom of the sea
has heaved its own tectonics
and nudged up through the surface of the earth
in all its sedimentary splendor

it is triumph despite the unbearable gravity of
being
we make way
with pocketfuls of shiny shards
with palmfuls of question marks
with bellyfuls of crackling chrysalis glistening

glittering

(from the chapbook *glistening, glittering*)

# Among the Tufa

In one aeon,
the sentinels
have risen up
from the salty azure waters,
and crouch, ready to spring up
along the shore. Warped,
craggy and roman-colored,
they warm underneath
the hesitant touch
of our
carefully placed fingers
as we navigate
our way through the
stately columns. Their pumice
surface bleeds us
dry of inarticulated rage,
preparing us for the silence
that descends like a twilight
upon our souls.

Nothing can
be heard, and I fear I've gone
deaf, though I can sense the
palpable beat of waves
on the shore, the brush of birds'
wings against the wind, the
weave of your jacket against
my arm. You nurse the
wintery injury on your right hand,
gone numb from a recent

impulse to satisfy your fledgling
curiousity. Our eyes meet, and I
hear the whisper of your smile
echo around us, and
I cease to be afraid.

We sit on a bench
and watch the sun hike
over the Sierras, as
the birds slice
through the air on invisible
whims. Our time for
solitude is drawing to a close,
but our peace remains
undisturbed, even as we backtrack
to your vehicle and depart
a little more wistful than we came.

# Embroidered

When pleated, I fold into the thinnest
slits. Garment without zippers, backed with basting,
smooth thread. To my hems tatted lace covers knit-
stitched skin. Plastic buttons — taut to my
cloth — grasp
at cotton like claws.
                    I imagine myself
the patterned product of a great seamstress: full-
length gown born of deft hands, I could adorn like
camisoles slim, white bodies.
                    Instead, my size
has been mis-measured and I am of no use.
Un-proportioned fit, I hang in the closet
bulky and bulged as an overcoat.

## Stone Walls

I came from cold Sweden
To cold New England
To farm this glacier-littered soil

For each seedling I plant
I must extract a stone from the ground
I'll add the stone to this elf-wall
What matter if the walls never meet?
Only fairies will dance them
Dogs nor horses they'll not keep in—
I use no mortar

Nothing holds my family together
We deserted kin and friends
What place we had, we left
We came to this land
Where we sleep over strangers' ancestors' bones
This land of extinguished futures

Did we come because we had hope
Or because we had no hope?

We know enough English now
To know they call us longheads
How surprised they were to discover
We were not idiots

This nation wet-nursed me
With stale milk
I am grateful not to go hungry

I know well whose backs are broken
To build railroads, mine coal

When I tire of farming rocks
The quiet woods will grow back
My meager progeny will scatter
You will see no more trace of
Me than these stone walls

127

# Long

1.

A singular surprise
with a sheepish tap
at my door;

I found the twist
of your ankle
lovely,

the knock of your knees
endearing.

You said,
"I tried to leave
but I missed you
already."

My relief was
insurmountable.

Strange,
we didn't hug
or rush into each
other's arms.

I nodded.

You entered.

We sat side by side
in exhausted silence
on the couch
all afternoon.

When sleep intruded,
we threw a cushion
on the den floor,
embraced one another
for warmth,

the harshness of the carpet
somehow appropriate
on the last honest night
of our lives together.

2.

I stand next to you
enduring
the endless parade
of conciliatory
congratulations.

My cousin,
Kenny the Jeweler,
set the tear shaped diamond
I bought in Veracruz
into the platinum band
free of charge.

Your father resembled
the gray ghost
of the stoic Indian,

more wrinkles on his brow
than the saddest Shar-Pei
in history.

Disconsolate fixed smiles
for the gay photographer,

sharp brayish laughter
when Nana's wheelchair
tore your watteau train,

these are the retrospect
memories fabricated
from second-guessed
afterthoughts.

Did we gleefully scamper
through a hazy sea
of blown soap bubbles?

Our tattooed Mercedes Benz
had gray plush leather seats;

Three cans of Dinty Moore
and four of Iams dog food
were securely tied to the

130

undercarriage,

your "something borrowed,"
an emergency tampon
from your mom,

and the new inflated appraisal
of the assembled ring you kept,

never knowing
the stone's true worth
and origin.

3.

*Long is the boredom*
*of the bible boy,*

*the dreams of a flower girl—*

*Short,*
*the first slice of cake.*

*Long is the zipper*
*of your wedding gown,*

*the aisle of the church—*

*Short,*
*the intermezzo of our vows.*

Long (and longer still)
was the year after our
last sincere night together,

when turbid hope withered
into the pluvial empyrean,

when masqueraded
lovemaking
became an unsolved
gangland slaying,

please arrest
the culprits responsible
the brokenhearted cry out.

Long is my sentence,
this innate inability
to forgive,

Short (and quick)
my expulsion
from Eden.

# Like Rotten Tongue

Like a poem by Seamus Heaney,
wormed and hungry;
like a sanguine complexion
well past ripe;
like the gleeful butcher
brooming blood in the gutter;
like so many flies
on heaps of butter.

Like insidious similes
in the hands of surgeons;
like hard-boiled egg
in a beggar's beard;
like a mother's mouth
wishing death to her daughter;
like rotten tongue;
like slaughter.

# Luis Rodriguez: poet, journalist, and activist (part 1)

There are very few artists who have accomplished as much as Luis Rodriguez. A poet (now nominated for California Poet Laureate), author, journalist, activist, publisher (Tia Chucha Press), and co-founder (along with his wife Trini and two other partners) of Tia Chucha Cafe & Centro Cultural; a bookstore, coffee house, art and workshop center in Sylmar. Luis took some time from his busy schedule to sit down and discuss his views on poetry, the art of writing, and the future of the L.A. poetry scene.

(Note: this inteview took place in February 2005, so some of the events mentioned herein have already taken place.)

*ML: How did you get involved in the poetry scene?*
LR: In L.A., I started about 25 years ago, in high school. I didn't know it yet, but I wrote little poetic vignettes. I started going to workshops in East L.A., the L.A. Latino Writers Workshop. That is where I really learned what poetry is about. There were a lot of great writers there: Victor Valle, who became a Pulitzer Prize winning journalist, Susan Mena, who was also a journalist, Louisa Nortes, and Eric Gamboa. They had a group called the Barrio Writers Workshop. They held workshops in East L.A., Echo Park, and even in the prisons. We started

134

doing poetry readings at Self-Help Graphics. I ended up becoming the director of the group in the early '80's. I then became the editor of the magazine, *XismeArte*.

When I got to Chicago, I already had that history, and I got there at the right time. The poetry slams had just barely gotten started. Then I really got into the poetry scene. I got active, and started a poetry press (Tia Chucha,) and worked with the Chicago Poetry Festival.

*ML: Why did you found Tia Chucha Press?*

LR: In Chicago, art and poetry were coming out everywhere; in the bars, the cafes, the libraries. Every night there were two or three venues where people were doing poetry, and I went to all of them, and read.

There was no press in Chicago covering the scene. I started by publishing my book (*Poems Across the Pavement*) first, in '89. I got money from the University of Chicago to do that, and it got a lot of attention. People started buying the book. So over the next two years, I published mostly Chicago poets: Patricia Smith, who became the International Slam Champion several times over; Michael Warr; David Hernandez, who was the main Puerto Rican poet at the time. He had a street sound with music and poetry.

135

*AUP: And Marc Smith?*

LR: We didn't publish Marc Smith. We worked with Marc, I knew him from early on.

Tia Chucha has published over 40 books and a CD. And it's not just Chicago poets, we publish from all over.

*AUP: How much diversity is there in the authors you publish?*

LR: We started off with a lot of diversity. The poetry scene in Chicago is very "democratic" in that sense. I have the feeling the poetry scene in L.A. is very segregated. The Chicanos had East L.A., and there were a lot of white poeple at Beyond Baroque. There was stuff coming out of South Central and other places, but it was all seperated into where people met.

In Chicago, it was all mixed; Chicanos, Puerto Ricans, African-Americans, and the rest, and so I started publishing right away. Michael Warr, Patricia Smith and Rohan Preston are African-American. David Hernandez is Puerto-Rican. Jean Howard is Anglo. Lisa Buscani is also Anglo. We publish the gamut of the best in the poetry scene. I've been doing it since I brought the press back to L.A.

*ML: Why did you move back to Sylmar, and not*

136

*East L.A.?*

LR: I moved back in December 2000, to Pacoima, because my wife Trini grew up and still had family there. We lived in the house she grew up in. My family had scattered from the East L.A. area.

We realised the North East Valley is a neglected area. This is the Mexican side of the valley, 80% Mexican and Central American. There was nothing here culturally; no bookstores, no movie houses, no art galleries, there was nothing. 400,000 people live here, and there was nothing going on.

We thought this would be a good venue, even though I got friends in South Central and East L.A. who said, "Why don't you start something down here?"

In the future we might, but right here is where we are going to keep Tia Chucha going and growing.

*ML: We'll you've done a great job. I like the space, it's very warm and welcoming.*

*You're a journalist and a poet. I heard you read at Los Angeles City College in 1993, at Beyond Baroque and The Midnight Special Bookstore. How does your role as a journalist affect you as a poet and novelist?*

LR: These are two different writing streams. Contradictory streams, but I think I've been able to make them work.

In journalism, you have to have an eye for detail, and use concrete language. In poetry, you get a chance to tap into emotional resonance. You can use and play with the musicality of language. Somehow, in my writing, both happen. I have a journalistic eye, but I have a lot of musicality in my words. I have been able to put both of them together, especially in my creative writing, like non-fiction and short stories.

Sometimes, I think it hurts people who don't know which way to go when they are doing both, but it comes together for me.

*ML: What circumstances led you to write the collection of short stories,* The Republic of East L.A.? *I've been online at Amazon and the book has gotten a lot of great reviews.*

LR: All of my work is autobiographical. My poetry and even my children's books are autobiographical. I finally decided to imagine people.

Now *The Republic of East L.A.* is written like real stories but I imagined them, and I couldn't do that for the longest time. My memoir (*Always Running*), and my poetry were based on everything I had experienced.

On my own I started to write short stories. I had a whole number of them before I decided I was capable of doing it. The first short story was a little too stuck in reality, and I kept working at it. Finally I got to the point where the characters had a life of their own. You know, how a character develops in their own little story, and how they carry you through their lives. That began to happen with my short stories.

Now, I have a novel coming out in April, my first fiction novel.

*AUP: What is the name of your novel?*

LR: It's called *The Music of the Mill*. It's about three generations of a Chicano family in a steel mill in L.A.

I worked in a steel mill for a number of years, so it's kind of going back to that time, but re-imagining everything and characters coming alive and completing themselves...it's amazing when it happens.

*AUP: There is nothing autobiographical in* Republic of East L.A.*?*

LR: There is a lot. Some of the characters I know personally, as well of some of the incidents with some of the people. But, what happens - again - is I started off with something I saw, or felt, then it went completely off on its own.

In the first story "My Ride, My Revolution,"

there actually was a limo drive who brought a limo into the barrio of Boyle Heights. But that was the only bit that was true. That character was completely made up, and I then imagined what the limo driver was like, and where he was working. That's the beauty of it. You get something real, and then it goes beyond that.

*ML: You're a poet, journalist, editor, publisher. You started Tia Chucha to support the art community in San Fernando Valley. When do you find the time to write?*

LR: Well, I have a lot of help. People volunteer. Tia Chucha has volunteer editors. The non-profit center next door has volunteers and volunteer resident artists. There is even a volunteer board.

My wife Trini helps a lot to run things. It's not like I'm doing everything by myself. I have a vision, I have inititiative. I get the money, and try to get the outreach. But people embrace it and take it on, so I don't really have to make that happen. I do have to with my writing. Nobody can do that for me.

My writing is like a job, from 9-5. I have the luxury where I work at home.

I'm gone 80-100 days a year, traveling. When I'm at home, I work on the computer. I try to write 2-3 hours a day, enough to get something going. Right now, I'm working on some essays. I have a short story in the works, and some other book projects.

*AUP: So, writing is your main vocation?*
LR: That's what I do.

*AUP: Not like the rest of us poets who have to work a job.*
LR: No, I know. It took a me a long time, I used to work two or three jobs and write on the side. But now, it's what I do.
Actually, the side things for me are Tia Chucha, the non-profit center, the press, and my other book that is coming out this spring. My focus is the writing.

*AUP: Congratulations.*
LR: I've got another poetry book coming out in the fall. It's called *My Nature is Hunger*.

*ML: Is it being published by Tia Chucha?*
LR: No. It's being published by Curbstone Press. They've published three of my books.

*AUP: Who are some of your influences?*
LR: They run the gamut. Pablo Neruda is my favorite poet. I love John Steinbeck, and Theodore Dreiser. I also like the work of John Fante, T.C. Boyle, and Sherman Alexi.

141

*AUP: Sherman Alexi is a great writer.*
LR: Reading a lot of great writers is a very important part of writing.

*ML: How do you feel about the poetry scene as a whole?*
LR: I think as a whole, the scene has the same problem as L.A. in that it's fractured. But, I think it's a very vibrant scene. The poets I've seen here and on your website are very strong young people with a lot of wonderful ways of saying things, Ariel Robello being one of them. It's a vibrant scene, but scattered.

The beauty about Chicago is that it's a compact city. Everybody gets to know each other. You get to see everybody at all the venues. Here, it's not that way.

I think Beyond Baroque, especially since the early '80's, was what I felt oriented to the white community. I think it's a vital institution, and it's been the center for the poetry scene for so long. But, hopefully we are creating a vital scene here too.

We have an open-mic here. Some nights have been amazing, some nights only a few people show up. We've had some amazing young people get up and read. We're a little corner of the scence, but it's fractured. Who's going to go out and get these people? It's just

142

the nature of the city. I don't think it's bad or good, it's just the way it is.

In the early '80's, I thought it was more egregated. I think things have come together much better now.

*ML: That's definitely true. And you've certainly done your part in making that happen. Angel told me almost a year ago that you had built this great place and were holding these readings, and I thought, "Wow, that is so cool." and I knew that it was going to be something good.*

*One of my goals for* poeticdiversity *is to try and get to those areas, those enclaves to come together more into the mainstream.*

*AUP: I call it "Uniting all the little Balkan States."*

LR: Actually, that's what it is.

*ML: What suggestions would you to further the involvement of bi-lingual poets, either in this area, or in other areas to become more a part of the L.A. poetry community?*

LR: I think we need to have a strong L.A. poetry festival. I know there has been a poetry festival, but I think one that can really reach out, maybe more central to downtown L.A., not just the Westside, but to people all over.

There is a lot of poetry happening that people don't even know about, like in the Pico-Union area, South Central, and East L.A.

143

There is a strong need to galvanize all the poets, put them together, and hear all the voices; Spanish, English, Korean, Armenian. You know, just really mix it up.

I don't know if anyone has the vision, the money, or even the interest, but that's what L.A. can do. It can have a vital, wonderful festival that can encompass all the things going on. Again, I don't want to put down the festival that does exist, I've never been to it. It's probably great, but more needs to happen.

*ML: That's interesting. The L.A. Poetry Festival is a month-long event. They have a series of more established readings, but all kinds of venues get sponsored. I co-host a reading in Santa Monica, the Rapp Saloon, and when the L.A. poetry festival comes around, we get fifty readers who wouldn't typically show up. It's also the one time of year where you get to see any cross-section of L.A. poets.*

LR: Then it would need to build on that, and I wouldn't want to say it's a bad thing. The festival is obviously important, but maybe more can be built up further.

*AUP: They bring in a lot of names from out of town to get a bigger draw. My criticism is there are a lot of local writers who are established that are*

144

*strong enough to make the festival happen on its own.*

LR: And that is what I think helped the Chicago poetry festival, which no longer exists, by the way. When we did it, we brought in only Chicago poets. It was a day-long event, not a month-long one.At its height we had 3,000 people show up at the Navy Pier to hear poet, after poet, after poet. We had poets like Gwendolyn Brooks. She was like the Mother-Goddess of Chicago poetry for everybody.

*ML: There's an environmental festival called Worldfest in April (2005). One part of Worldfest is an all-day poetry reading, and I'd like to ask you: Who would you reccomend to feature? I have a chance to fill four slots, and I got one left.*
LR: Ariel Robello would be the one.

*ML: I already asked her. She's on tour until June.*
LR: I think a lot of the young people around here need more development. I did some poetry workshops, but I want to continue to get them to learn more about poetry performance.
I think that is what people need. To me, the Chicago poetry scene was like school. People didn't see it that way, but you got schooled in language, performance, and the music of

words.It was a very hopeful kind of thing.
we don't have that here yet?

*AUP: Did you go to school in Chicago?*
LR: No, I lived there for fifteen years. I worked there. I mean "school," in the sense of learning, by watching people.
I think one good thing L.A. has is the *L.A. Times* Festival of Books. I've been to so many book festivals, and that is one of the best.

*AUP: They have a poetry pavillion.*
*ML: There's another; the DIY (Do It Yourself) Book Festival. I went last October (2004), and it's almost as big a draw as the* L.A.Times *Book Festival, and it's for small presses.*
LR: Where is it?

*ML: In West Hollywood, near the Pacific Design Center. I think this year it will take place in September.*
LR: I've been there the last couple of years, on panels.

*AUP: Have you ever been to the Shouting Coyote Festival?*
LR: No.

*AUP: They have two seperate stages for poets. Some poets perform on both, it's not organized by the*

146

*same people, but I like it.*
LR: No kidding, that's great. Where is it?

*AUP: In Sunland-Tujunga. The reason I asked if
you went to school in Chicago - street poetry
versus academic poetry. How do you balance it?*
LR: I'm not an academic poet. There's just no
way around it. I can't say that I am.
I think the battle of the so-called "us versus
them" is totally contrived. Good poetry
comes from many different places. There are
great poets from the street, whereever that
might be, performing and there's some great
academic poets.
Somebody else had decided that there's two
different worlds here. I don't know, because
I'm not an academic poet, I don't come from
there, but I do read so many poets, and some
of them are academic. A lot of their stuff is
amazing; I like it when the words happen in
a way that only "this" person could have
done it, and something magical begins to
happen. It doesn't matter to me where it
comes from.
Academic poets is have more time to analyze,
deconstruct, and workshop their poetry. If
you are a street poet, sometimes it happens
when you make it happen, but I think it
shows that anybody, academic or not, has
poetry in them. That's the main thing, that

147

there is poetry in everyone, and there are ways to tap into that poetry. I do it in juvenile facilities, homeless shelters, migrant camps, prisons, public schools, whereever. And you know, all these people say,"These kids aren't poetic," and I have them doing things they wouldn't have thought they could do, and I have them writing amazing things.

So, there is kind of a false dichotomy in a certain sense. On the other hand, I always thought people who have money could go to school and learn. To me there is a class relationship to that. There's nothing wrong with them if they can do it, but there's no reason to look down on anyone else who doesn't have it. You know what I mean. Poetry should be for everybody.

*AUP: That leads me to my next question.I've noticed Latino, Hispanic poetry in particular, gets more attention when it's socially conscious. What's wrong with just quality Hispanic poetry without including the aspect I just mentioned?*

LR: It runs both ways. Like for example, my poetry does. When I came into the Chicano Movement, there was a lot of interest to speak to your reality, which prompted us, in many ways to become poets. We wanted to find a language to address the issues that we were facing. But the more you develop as a poet, pretty soon you are writing love songs or writing to your kid. So if you look at my poetry and at Chicano poetry, you'll see it runs the gamut. It's true a lot of the initial impulse of Chicano poetry was that movement, but I think it's also how people developed. I wouldn't be against anybody writing about the rain versus a cop beating up a kid in the street. They're both areas for poetry to come out of, but the movement created what we call Chicano poetry.

It's different for other Latinos. It all depends. Puerto Ricans ar very much like that, they came out of the same movement. I found a lot of Cuban-American writers didn't seem to have the same impetus, necessarily. So many of them developed quality poems about other subjects, you know, about their lives, except in relation to Castro.

Your environment gives you the pallate to write with.

Bio: Luis Rodriguez is convinced that a writer can change the world. Indeed it is through education and the power of words that Rodriguez saw his own way out of the barrio of East L.A. and successfully broke free from the years of violence and desperation he spent as an active gang member. Achieving success as an award-winning Chicano poet, he was sure the streets would haunt him no more — until his young son joined a gang himself. Rodriguez fought for his child by telling his own story in the bestseller *Always Running: La Vida Loca, Gang Days in L.A.*, a vivid memoir that explores the motivation of gang life and cautions against the death and destruction that inevitably claim its participants.

Rodriguez is also known for helping start a number of prominent organizations — such as Chicago's Guild Complex, one of the largest literary arts organizations in the Midwest, and the small poetry publishing house, Tia Chucha Press. He is also one of the founders of Youth Struggling for Survival, a Chicago-based not-for- profit community group working with gang and non-gang youth. Along with his wife, Trini, and brother-in-law Enrique Sanchez, Luis is co-founder of Tia Chucha's Café & Centro Cultural—a bookstore, coffee shop, art gallery, performance space, and workshop center in Los Angeles. Rodriguez conducts workshops, readings, and talks in juvenile detention facilities, migrant camps, universities, and public and private schools. Rodriguez addresses the complex but vital issues of race, class, gender, and personal rage through dialogue, story, poetry, and art.

An accomplished poet, Luis Rodriguez is the author of several collections of poetry, including *Poems Across the Pavement*, *The Concrete River*, and *Trochemoche*. His poetry has won a Poetry Center Book Award, a PEN/Josephine Miles Literary Award, and *ForeWord* magazine's Silver Book Award, among others. His books for children, *America Is Her Name* and *It Doesn't Have To Be This Way: A Barrio Story*, are published in both English and Spanish. Considered by the American Libraries Association as one of the nation's 100 most censored books, his work *Always Running* earned a Carl Sandburg Literary Award and was designated a *New York Times* Notable Book. Luis Rodriguez is also author of *Hearts and Hands: Creating Community in Violent Times* and a short story collection, *The Republic of East LA : Stories.* His first novel, *Music of the Mill* (Rayo Books/HarperCollins), was published in May 2005. His fourth poetry collection is *My Nature is Hunger* (Curbstone Press, fall 2005). Luis Rodriguez was one of 50 leaders worldwide selected as "Unsung Heroes of Compassion," presented by the Dalai Lama.

## Editor At Large: A Poet's Perspective:
## *Next...Magazine /Poetix's*
## G. Murray Thomas

*pd: You founded* Next Magazine *in 1994. What circumstances led to the founding of* Next?

GMT: There once was a publication called *OutLoud*, a four page listing of all the poetry events around L.A. The people who put it out passed it out at poetry readings every month. But, as happens with such projects, they eventually ran out of energy and resources, and ceased publication. It left a huge gap in the SoCal poetry scene.

At the time I was trying to establish Orange Ocean Press as a viable poetry publisher. Larry Schulz, who was helping me with that, suggested we do something like *OutLoud*. Somehow I let him convince me that was a good idea. But I wanted to do more than just a calendar. I wanted a full magazine about the poetry scene, with reviews and commentary. So that's what we started.

*pd: What is the biggest difference between the Los Angeles poetry scene then and now?*

GMT: Before I started *Next* there was a lot of geographic segregation in the SoCal poetry scene. Poets stuck with their local reading, because that was all they knew about. During the four years I published *Next*, I was able to watch the scene come together, watch poets from across SoCal become aware of each other, and interact with each other.

Since *Next* folded, I have noticed some of the old segregation creeping back in. But the poets who want to know what's going on elsewhere are finding out. There are still plenty of resources to find out about poetry, starting, but not nearly limited to, *Poetix*.

A major change I've seen, even since we folded, has been an increase in the variety of poetry readings. While the basic coffeehouse open/ featured reading is still the norm, poetry readings take many other forms these days. There are much larger readings than there were when I started; Da Poetry Lounge at the Greenway Court Theater on Fairfax gets 200+ every Tuesday night. There are people producing real poetry shows--a selection of featured readers designed to entertain an non-poet audience; John Hemsley's FlyPoet Showcase puts on such a show every month. And then there are boundary-pushing events like Rachel Kann's Co-lab:oration, where poets are required to collaborate in their performances, either with other poets or with the musicians Rachel provides. The result is one of the most exciting, adventurous poetry readings around. And even the old coffeehouse readings are often produced far more professionally than they ever were in the past.

pd: *What has remained constant?*
GMT: Hundreds of poets eager for their five minutes on the mike.

pd: *What has been most surprising and unexpected?*
GMT: Ten years ago I was convinced poetry and spoken word were poised to be the next big thing in popular culture, that by now, poetry CDs would be at least making the charts, if not topping them, that poets would be headlining tours of big venues. Again, maybe not Staples Center, but at least the Wiltern. I am somewhat surprised that that hasn't happened. Poetry certainly has a higher profile in popular culture than it has had in years, if ever in America, but it's still a sideshow.

pd: *You successfully published* Next *for quite a few years. Why did you decide to merge* Next *with* Poetix?
GMT: There are different types of success. *Next* was a success as far as reaching its intended audience, helping connect the SoCal poetry scene, and, to a certain extent, as a vehicle for critical discussion.
However, it was never a financial success. I lost

money on it every year. Eventually I had lost far more money than I could afford to lose, and had't give up.

As for the merge with *Poetix*, that actually came a couple years after I had ceased publication of *Next*. I was still maintaining a calendar, primarily on my Web page. Larry Jaffe was starting *Poetix*, and he asked me about combining our efforts. I immediately agreed, because what he was doing with *Poetix* was similar to what I had done with Next, only on the Web instead of in print. (We were hoping to create a print version of *Poetix*, but we still haven't found the funding to do that.)

*pd: As a publisher and an editor, what are some of your likes/dislikes?*

GMT: What I'm looking for in poetry, as an editor and as a poetry fan, are poems that grab me and entertain me when I first hear them, and then continue to reveal more depth and meaning when I read them on the page.

I definitely prefer imagery over flat statement. Give me something to see, and make me think about what you're saying.

I think my main dislike, especially at readings, is "poetry" which has been not worked over. Journal entries, "I just wrote this five minutes ago," and all that.

Just because you wrote your ideas down in short lines doesn't make them a poem. Much of this stuff is material for poetry, but it takes work to turn an idea into a poem.

I'll admit that I try pieces out at open readings to see how they work in performance, but that's a late step in my writing, not an initial one.

Once I feel I can't improve a poem just by more rewriting, I'll read it to an audience, and that often gives me a better idea of what's working and what's not especially what parts of it are clumsy.

*pd: As an editor, what advice would you give poets to improve the quality of their literary evolution?*

GMT: First the obvious. Read other poets. Listen to other poets. Notice what works in their poetry. You don't have to try to sound like other poets, but you should understand how their poems work. That will help your own writing.

And, as implied in my answer above—rewrite. Rewrite everything; even if it's perfect already, at least try it a different way. I'm fully aware some poems come out fully formed right away. But most need some work and if you never rewrite anything, you won't know which ones are done and which

156

aren't.

But if you get in the habit of rewriting, then you will know when something is perfect the first time.

*pd: How do you see* Poetix *evolving over the next five years?*

GMT: Organically. We have all sorts of dreams and wishes for *Poetix*, including a print version, but what actually happens with it is going to depend on who comes forward to help, what they want to do, what they are able to do. (Hint, hint, we always need volunteers. And what would really help *Poetix* grow and evolve would be someone to sell ads).

*pd: How does your role as a poet and musician affect your role as publisher/editor?*

GMT: It was my immersion in the scene as a poet that inspired me to try publishing. I started publishing as an attempt to create an audience for poets I heard who I thought would appeal to people who generally didn't read poetry.

I planned a series of poetry anthologies on "unpoetic" subjects. The first was surfing, the second pollution. Unluckily, a planned third anthology, on laundromats, never happened. I also published books by Larry Schulz and

Tom Foster, and a book of poetic cartoons by Santa Barbara's Walt Hopmans. I have published two chapbooks of my own on my Orange Ocean Press, but I did not start publishing to publish myself.

By being a part of the scene, I was able to find many poets I wanted to publish without having to solicit material.

*pd: Karen Corcoran Dabkowski, the poetry editor for* The Blue House *once observed, "Music bypasses a good deal of the cerebral and cuts straight to the visceral in ways poetry cannot. It's the difference between swallowing a capsule that slowly digests in your system and mainlining heroin."*

*As a poet and musician, what are your thoughts on this statement?*

GMT: To a great degree I agree with it. You don't have to think about music to enjoy it. In fact, thinking about it can take away from the enjoyment.

When I started combining my poetry with music, I noticed a few things. The first was how my own relationship with my words changed. Adding the music forced me to change my delivery of my poetry. In a way, it freed me from certain delivery patterns I had gotten locked into from over use.

At the same time, adding the music

deemphasized the importance of the words. I often found myself on stage with the band, reciting a poem, and wondering if anyone was even listening to the words, or if they were only hearing the music.

*pd: I f you could select only one book and one music CD, what would they be for the following situations/places:*
*1) Road trip through the desert:*
GMT: Music (if I'm not allowed to bring my own mix tapes, I need my mix tapes when driving): *Substance*, by New Order. Book: *Turtle Island*, by Gary Snyder.

*2) Bachelor party:*
GMT: Music: *Led Zeppelin II* (get the testosterone raging). Book: Who's going to be reading at a bachelor party?

*3) Los Angeles:*
GMT: Music: Any Doors album. Book: *Day of the Locust*, by Nathaniel West or *Play It As It Lays*, by Joan Didion.

*4) New York City:*
GMT: Music: *Marquee Moon*, by Television. Book: *Gravity's Rainbow*, by Thomas Pynchon. Although it's not about New York, it has that frenzied, crowded, urban feel I

associate with New York.

*5) Walden Pond (the location):*
GMT: Music: *Forest*, by George Winston. Book: Boy, it would be easy to say *Walden*, wouldn't it? But I'm going to go with *Tao of Physics*, by Fritoj Capra. While you're contemplating nature, you might as well be contemplating the nature of nature. Although, equally good with just be the *I Ching*.

*6) Waking from a nightmare:*
GMT: Music: *Kind of Blue*, by Miles Davis. Book: *Pogo* or *Calvin & Hobbes*.

*pd: Who are some of your literary influences, both classical and contemporary?*
GMT: My favorite classic poet is William Carlos Williams. I love the way he turned ordinary language poetic. But even better than Williams, in my opinion, is his publisher, James Laughlin. He's one of the unsung heroes of modern poetry. He founded and ran New Directions, which is responsible for probably half the great poets of the mid-20th century, and he was a truly awesome poet himself.
But most of the real influences on my poetry are contemporary and local. People I've heard at

poetry readings around town. This was
especially true when I was first writing
poetry 15 years ago. I definitely learned my
(current) style from listening to other poets,
seeing what they did. Poets like Eric Brown,
Gary Tomlinson, and Ron de la Rosa all had
a great influence on me. I think the main
thing I learned was to push my poems, to
make them fully alive.
Another major influence has been song lyrics.
While I rarely write actual songs (my sense
of rhythm is just plain off, and a song needs
a steady beat), I learned the value of a great
line from rock songs.

*pd: You are dedicated, compassionate, and
enthusiastic. It's reflected in your poetry, and in
your contributions to the poetry scene. Has your
dedication/compassion/enthusiasm for poetry,
music, and art in general ever waned to the point
what you considered taking up another vocation?*
GMT: No. Writing is what gives my life
meaning (and how I find meaning in my life,
if you can see the difference). I've always
structured my life, and chosen my jobs, so I
could write. While I have yet to actually
make a living at it, it remains the most
important thing in my life.
I have found that successful creation has a
greater effect on my mood, day to day, and

long term, than anything else I can think of (except maybe romance).

*pd:Your poem "Cows on the Freeway" invokes this thought: Our world is increasingly high tech and lowbrow. What does this thought invoke for you?*
GMT: The technology itself has no effect on what people use it for. It may make it easier for people to fulfill their taste, whatever it may be, but ithas minimal influence on that taste. The Internet makes it easier to find porn, for those who want that (and apparently plenty do.) But it also makes it easier to discover obscure bands, or spoken word recordings, or view classical art, if that's your taste.
I think something like this can be seen in poetry today. Poetry itself is about as low tech an enterprise as you could imagine. All you need is yourself, your mind to think it up and your mouth to deliver it. But the vitality of the poetry scene today owes much to technology, especially the Internet. You can find a poetry reading near you, or set up a national poetry tour, or just read someone's poetry on the Internet. Poets across the country, and even the globe, are linked together through it. I find out what's going on in poetry all across the country just by reading my e-mail. The level of networking

162

among poets right now is amazing, especially when compared to as short as ten years ago.

That's not even mentioning all the ways technology enables poets to get their work out there. Starting with desktop publishing, and all the zines and chapbooks that has enabled. Then there's publishing on the Web, both e-zines like *poeticdiversity*, and individual poet's Web pages. Plus home recording and burning of CDs. The avenues for publication and distribution are huge because of technology.

Of course, none of this has more than an indirect effect on the quality of the work being produced. Hopefully, with it so easy to find poetry today, poets are reading and listening to more other poets, and learning their craft that way.

Unluckily, self-publishing has removed the filter of an editor, and a lot of crap is getting published this way. Which kind of goes back to the beginning of my answer here—the explosion of art available makes it more important that the reader, viewer and/or listener has some taste of their own. It requires them to sort through what's out there to find the good stuff.

*pd: You have a poetry show on KBEACH. How is*

*that working out for you?*

GMT:Very well. I've been able to get some great poets on the air, Rachel Kann, Matthew Niblock, Raindog, Jaimes Palacio and many others. We chat about their poetry, and what they're doing these days, and they read some poems.

The strange thing about radio is I never have a clue how many, if any, people are listening. It's performance in a vacuum.

*pd: What other projects do you have in the works right now?*

GMT: I'm working on a novel right now. That's where most of my writing energy is going.

I am also trying to republish *Paper Shredders*, an anthology of surf writing I put out 12 years ago. It was the first book I published on Orange Ocean Press, which eventually morphed into Next.

Anyway, I always liked the work in *Paper Shredders*, and felt that if I could have had wider distribution, it could have sold quite well. So that's what I'm working on right now, getting that wider distribution for it.

Bio: G. Murray Thomas is best known as the editor of *Next... Magazine*, a poetry calendar/newsmagazine for Southern California. *Next... Magazine* was published monthly between 1994 and 1998. Thomas currently puts out the *Next... Calendar*, a monthly listing of poetry events. His latest project is MURRAY, a garage jazz/spoken word band. In MURRAY, Thomas performs his poetry over improvised musical backing. Thomas' first full length collection of poems, *Cows on the Freeway*, was published by iUniverse in 2000. He has also published four chapbooks, *Death to the Real World*, *Opposite Oceans*, *Poetry Spilled All Over the Carpet* and *A Rare Thing*. Thomas has performed his poetry all over Southern California, at almost every major poetry venue. He has also performed at Lollapalooza, The Whiskey, The Coach House and the 1996 National Poetry Slam.

## my muse speaks

...yea, verily;
the sufis advise:
"when you come upon truth,
say not; 'i have found THE truth,'
rather say instead;
'i have found A truth',
or; just
shut
up"

    as I lay abed on a recent hot summer nite,
sneezing into a large volume of kant, i was
visited by my own personal poetry muse
'berato', who arrived, as was her usual M.O., in
a wisp of smoke smelling of opium & lilac.

    she perched herself upon a large pile of dirty
laundry in the corner near the mattress & lit a
small cigar.

    "lissin kid', [she often called me kid,] "in spite
of what you might stumble across in the
writings of dusty old europeans, poetry today is
not what it always has been."

    "how can that be?', i asked, '"for isnt the
observation & celebration of beauty, as an order
transcending specifics & therefore all instances
of subjective feeling, the standard by which any
writing, sculpture, or painting, is adjudged as
art?"

    ...the muse smacked me solidly upside the
head with the flat of her hand, smiling sweetly.

166

"that's for using the word 'adjudged'. no
fuzz-nuts, i'm afraid the drivel you just spouted
is part of an out-moded ideal."

she pointed to my faded vinyl window blind
& an apparition appeared upon its cracked &
filthy surface:

a plumber wearing dingy brown cartharts
was sitting at a greasy lunch counter. he
swallowed a gulp of beer & burped, then
turned to us & said;

"plato's ideals were plato's; they don't pay
my rent, or float my boat."

with that, the apparition vanished.

"you know", said the muse, polishing her
fingernails on her toga, "ultimately, beauty is a
construct of the human mind, & is therefore
subjective to humans & NOT truly universal.
after all, earth could be the ugliest part of the
universe for all you posers know".

"so the appreciation of beauty in & of itself is
not only valid definition for what constitutes art
or poetry?", i ventured cautiously, wary of
another crack upon my cranium.

"did i stutter?" she asked arching an eyebrow.
"the way you humans see needs to be constantly
updated".

she pointed again to the window blind where
a vision of a lab coated scientist appeared. he
pushed a thick pair of glasses up the bridge of
his nose & said; "the more we find out; the less

we know", & shrugged sheepishly. the vision disappeared & the muse flicked cigar ashes on my rug.

"ideas of beauty change from culture to culture, from century to century. these changes are generally driven by the youth as old farts cling to old modes. granny hates the way kids these days talk & dance, & her granny felt the same way, & so on. academia & other establishment poobahs hear the wind blowing now & understand it later.

there have been & will be too many ideals of beauty to make it the sole standard for what art is & can ONLY be for the history & future of the human race.

the purpose & definition of art is more than upholding a standard of beauty. in fact, what i came tonite to lay down to you is the concept that art & poetry ought to be, among other things, the inspiring of new modes of perception in the observer & the thorough shaking of old ones"

"so what constitutes poetry?" i asked

"pay attention", she said, leaning forward & grasping my chin in her hand with a vise-like grip,

"poetry is word/craft & word/art.

craft is being thoughtful, clever & deliberate, & showing style. art is bringing together elements that shake-up peoples perceptions, &

offer new perspectives, ultimately inspiring the audience.

it's not just about meter & lyricism & upholding an antiquated ideal of beauty.

"what about the differences between written poetry & performed poetry?", i asked, hoping to not to piss her off by changing the subject.

she curled her lip & furrowed her brow.    "a good performance can smooth out mediocre writing, blurring it to the point where one can no longer trust that which one hears or, in some cases, trust that they're hearing anything at all. a performance poet is someone that disseminates poetry by performance, period. if you're reading it out loud, you're performing it. but before its performed, it has to be written. so all poetry must start, & ultimately stand on its merits there on the page. what's done with it after that is just window dressing."

"so... what is...poetry?", i asked, flinching & wincing, as she raised her hand again, then took a long drag off the cigar

"lissin close bean brain; a poem is: a literary endeavor of celebratory or descriptive expression, written with the aim of moving the audience thru its modes of expressed perception, & perspective"

"yes'm", i offered.

"now don't ever make me hafta fukkin tell you this again", she warned, & poofed away in a vapor of purple smoke.

i tossed kant into the corner & picked up a dog-eared copy of bukowski's 'mocking bird wish me luck'. i wondered if i had any more beer left.

# Review: Daniel Olivas' *Devil Talk: Stories*

Go ahead, call it magical realism. Although only half of the twenty-six stories in *Devil Talk: Stories* contain magical realist elements, Daniel A. Olivas is happy to share the label with writers like Isabel Allende, Kathleen Alcalá and Gabriel García Márquez.

Olivas is also part of an interesting trend, *cuentos de fantasmas*, or ghost stories, which blend Mexican folklore with American pop culture. Sounds very "X-Files" to me. Inspired by legends of El Diablo, his series of La Diabla tales interspersed throughout this collection are skillfully told as folk tales without sounding artificially folksy. One of these, "Don de la Cruz and the Devil of Malibu," also appears in the Rob Johnson anthology, *Fantasmas: Supernatural Stories by Mexican American Writers* (Bilingual Press/Editorial Bilingüe, 2001). The story happens to feature one of Olivas' characteristically brazen and compelling openings:

> *Don Jesús de la Cruz slept with the Devil. No, this is both too euphemistic and inaccurate. Don de la Cruz screwed the Devil, fucked the Devil, but never slept with the Devil, La Diabla. As most of us know, the Devil who lived in Southern California was a female, so she was La Diabla, not El Diablo. Because the Devil is legion, the Devil resides*

*in most towns and cities and may be a man or*
*a woman. It all depends on what is needed.*

Olivas' book is a page-turner, the work of a
master storyteller. Once I started the book, I
couldn't keep myself from reading it, mostly
during stoplights, as I drove through
Hollywood traffic on La Brea.

Many endings feature a twist. I won't give
anything away, but I should warn you that
these tales are not often wrapped up tidily with
a thorough explanation or resolution. You have
to maintain a tolerance for ambiguity and an
appreciation for the quality of a moment or an
image, even if you never find out what happens
next.

The collection entertains in its diversity like
an anthology or magazine. Olivas writes from
different points of view - first person narratives,
third person, and even second person - and
varies the tense depending on the needs of the
story. Some stories are brief sketches, others
elaborately plotted.

Like the magical realists, Olivas writes from
an outsider's perspective, though in Los
Angeles, Mexican-Americans are hardly a
"minority." With at least one Chicano character
in each story, the characters nevertheless
portray a broad range of Mexican-American
experience: from upwardly-mobile

professionals to farmworkers, from a convert to
Judaism to a drag queen. In "Willie," we get a
glimpse of a young man at the margins of his
community through the eyes of his open-
hearted little sister:

> *Wilfredo likes to dress to get Papá all
> riled up. You know, Willie wears those short-
> shorts that you see on the ladies who walk up
> and down that bad street near the Shell
> Station that Mamá says no self-respecting
> good Catholic would wander by unless your
> car died and you needed to get some help from
> Manny who works there. Mamá says those
> putas have no right to mess up our nice
> neighborhood. But the neighborhood don't
> look so nice and I figure some pretty ladies
> walking up and down a street can only make
> things look nice, right?*

In "Tabula Rasa" we meet a young couple
dealing with male/female dynamics within a
changing cultural context:

> *I wanted to grab her hands, stop them,
> squeeze them, and make her look at me while
> she told me what she did yesterday. But I
> didn't because she'd pull away, tell me not to
> be so macho, a typical male. A typical
> Mexican male. And then I'd say, no, I'm*

173

*Chicano and almost done with college. I'm no*
*Neanderthal. So instead of getting into a*
*stupid fight, I stood silently and let her finish*
*cleaning the desk.*

Olivas obviously lives observantly and his seemingly effortless characterizations are realistically complex. Personalities, even in the folkloric or fantastical stories, are depicted in natural and even earthy ways. For example, many of his characters are sexual beings, yet Olivas' writing is free of gratuitous sex scenes. Also blissfully absent are annoyingly shallow or stereotypical descriptions of female characters such as I encounter in a lot of men's work.

Most of the stories are set in Los Angeles, though some take place in today's L.A. while others occur back in the days of El Pueblo de Nuestra Señora La Reina de los Ángeles de la Porciúncula. Regardless of the historical setting, the characters ring true to their context.

Often one character speaks in Spanish while the other replies in English. I would imagine this yields an enjoyable, culturally-reinforcing experience for the bilingual/bicultural reader. As a mostly monolingual reader, I found Olivas' handling of language added a layer of disorientation, though to differing effect depending on the story. In some cases it enhanced the mood of ambiguity and uncertainty. In other cases it reflected the disorientation that's part of my daily reality, living and working among Spanish speakers here in L.A.

These characters dwell in overlapping worlds, from the matter-of-fact existence of Aztec and Christian deities to the universal inanity of the corporate office. This moment in the story "Monk" could fit neatly into a "Dilbert" cartoon or one of my favorite movies, "Office Space":

> *He remembered how on his first day at Caltrans, his new supervisor, Roland, told him his memos could be really "perked up" with such simple markings--"bullets," Roland called them.* **Bullets.** *Ever since then, Antonio used bullets in his memos. In fact, he became addicted to bullets particularly because the more he used, the more compliments he received from Roland.*

Later in the same story, Antonio experiences a family dynamic common to many cultures:

> *His mother tapped his arm and he turned to her. 'We only want the best for you,' she said. His father nodded.* How can they know what's best for me if I don't know what's best for me?

Olivas has numerous gifts as a writer, yet he uses his tools sparingly, not imposing a technique onto a story just because he's good at it. "Muy Loca Girl" reveals his talent for concise yet layered description in a tale that is full of contemplation like its protagonist, Marta:

> *Isabel's flat nose hovered above thick lips*
> *and reminded Marta of the Aztec carvings*
> *she studied in her ancient cultures textbook*
> *last year but never saw in person.*

Likewise, in "Bender," Olivas sets the tone for the story with poetic efficiency:

> *The Los Angeles summer sun shines*
> *hard and heartlessly through the large*
> *window and lights up the bed like a*
> *Broadway stage.*

Olivas' outlook in this approachable and hard-to-put-down collection is compassionate and optimistic. Perhaps not too surprising for an author whose day job is environmental law. A book like this makes me wish I were skilled at generating extravagant praise. It certainly merits it. It's a collection to be proud of, and I can't wait for his next book to come out. I'll just have to try not to read that one while driving.

(*Devil Talk: Stories* by Daniel A. Olivas. Bilingual
Press/Editorial Bilingüe, Tempe, Arizona. 2004.
$13.00)

177

# Bios

**Steve Abee** has published two books: *King Planet*, a collection of stories and poems, and *The Bus: Cosmic Ejaculations of the Daily Mind in Transit*, a novel. He also released a CD, titled *Jerusalem Donuts*, but that was a million years ago. He is currently working on a new novel, titled *Johnny Future*, and he has a poetry manuscript that is looking for a publisher.

He is a middle school English teacher, is married, has two daughters, and lives in Los Angeles.

**Neil Atkin** was born in 1974 in Vancouver, British Columbia, and raised in Saudi Arabia, Taiwan, the United States, and Canada. He has lived in a wide variety of communities: from small farming towns in northern Saskatchewan to the industrial districts of Taipei City. Over the course of his 30 years, he has been a farm laborer, an artist, a missionary, a university student, a math tutor, a computer games programmer, and now a graduate student.

Since moving to California, he has become an active participant and regular feature at many poetry readings throughout southern California. His work has appeared in *Inscape*, *Anagram*, and *Prairie Poetry*. He recently started work on an MFA in Creative Writing at UC Riverside where he serves as the assistant poetry editor of their new graduate journal, *CRATE*.

**Aurora Antonovic** is a Canadian writer and visual artist, and the former editor and columnist for the now-defunct *GT Times*. Her poetry has recently appeared in *Adagio Verse Quarterly*, *Poetic Voices*, *Promise*, *Black Mail Press*, *Above Ground Testing*, and *Poetry Super Highway*.
She currently acts as Canadian liaison for *Muse Apprentice Guild*.

**RD Armstrong** (Raindog to his friends) lives in a barrio in Long Beach, where he continues to publish some of the best poems written in this century in his magazine, *The Lummox Journal* and online at *DUFUS*. The curious may visit his website at http://home.earthlink.net/~lumoxraindog/. He also has a new book entitled *RoadKill (meditations on 9-11 and the American Wanderlust.)*

**Laura Golden Bellotti** is a writer and developmental book editor living in Los Angeles. Her poems won Honorable Mention in the National League of American Pen Women, San Francisco Branch, Poetry

Competition, and her poetry has appeared in *Poetic Medicine*, by John Fox (Tarcher/Putnam) and *Essential Love*, edited by Ginny Lowe Connors (Poetworks/Grayson Books), as well as in a number of literary journals, including *New Millennium Writings*; *CQ: California State Poetry Society Quarterly*; *Liberty Hill Poetry Review*; *Coracle Poetry*; and *Work: a Literary Journal*. Her recent chapbook is entitled *Angeleno Birch Tree Girl in the Land of Glare*.

Ms. Bellotti is the co-author of four nonfiction books: *Latina Power!* (Simon & Schuster, 2003); *Dr. Ana Nogales' Book of Love, Sex and Relationships: A Guide for Latino Couples* (Broadway Books/Bantam-Doubleday-Dell, 1998-99); *Creative Weddings* (Plume/Penguin, 1994); and *You Can't Hurry Love* (Dutton/Penguin, 1992). She was the developmental editor of the best-selling *Women Who Love Too Much* and has since edited numerous nonfiction books in the areas of creativity, psychology, relationships, women's issues, parenting, and health.

*The Holy Triangle: Stories of Pico-Robertson* is Ms. Bellotti's first collection of short stories.

**Julia Bemiss** is the associate editor for *poeticdiversity*. She hails from Ft. Wayne, Indiana and moved to Los Angeles in 1997.

Julia has been featured at The Velocity Cafe's "Horse of Another Color", Abbot's Habbit, and scored her first "10" while slamming at Da Poetry Lounge in 2004. Her work has appeared in *Pieces of Me: Voices of WriteGirl*, *getunderground.com*, and the anthology *L.A. Melange: the first year of poeticdiversity* (Sybaritic Press 2004.)

Julia graduated cum laude with academic honors in writing from Ball State University, in Muncie, Indiana. She likes to point out that she is a fan of David Letterman, who also graduated from Ball State.

**MC Bruce** works as an attorney with the Orange County Public Defender's Office. He is the single parent of a ten-year-old boy who is a remarkable soccer goaltender and drummer.

Mr. Bruce (the non-drumming father) has been published in a number of print and online journals, including *Rattle*, *Urban Spaghetti*, *Babylon*, and *ReMark*. He edits a small poetry journal, *The Blue Mouse*.

He's featured at many major Southern Calfornia venues and was a reader at a past San Luis Obispo Poetry Festival event. He also performs music around Southern California. He presently reviews books of poetry for *Ibbettson Street Newsgroup* and *Small Press*

*Review.*

**Troy P. Cárdenas** has an MFA in playwriting from UC San Diego and currently resides in Los Angeles. He loves steep hikes, wild flowers, his dog, Mediterranean food, Spain, France, the sun, very strong storms, day, and espcially night.

**Tobi Cogswell** is a poet from 4:00AM to 6:00AM. From 6:00AM to 9:00PM she is a worker bee, a mom, *and* a poet. From 9:00PM to 6:00AM she is hoping for inspiration for the next day. She is not crafty and cannot sew, but she will be glad to teach you to Greek dance or administer your retirement plan.

**Larry Colker** hails from West Virginia and currently resides in San Pedro. He co-hosts the weekly Redondo Poets reading at the Coffee Cartel in Redondo Beach, CA. He taught at USC before switching to technical writing for the software industry. His most recent collection of poetry is titled *What the Lizard Knows: New and Selected Poems.*

**Peggy Dobreer** is an educator, parent, poet, public speaker, and artisan.
She was a leading force in the educational vision of the Center for the Advancement of

182

Nonviolence, from 1997-2004, and co-wrote
and edited *64 Ways to Practice Nonviolence, A
Curriculum and Resource Guide*, published by
ProEd Publishers and distributed at
www.nonviolenceworks.com.

Her poetry has been published in *Cracked
Pavement and Plastic Trees: Our Gifts To
Future Generation, An Anthology of
Environmental Poetry, Everything About You Is
Beautiful: Really Big Show Anthology* (Winter
2004), *WordWright's Magazine, Tamafyhr
Mountain Irregular Poetry Journal,* and *The
Blue House.* She has self-published three
chapbooks: *Henceforth* (1999), *Bravo Collection*
(2002), and *Face of Sky* (2004). Peggy is a
contributing writer for *poeticdiversity.*

She has been featured at The Rapp Saloon, The
Coffee Cartel, and King's Cafe. Peggy is the
host of "A Horse of Another Color, Dinner
Poetry" at the Velocity Cafe, in Santa
Monica, CA.

**Francisco J. Dominguez** emigrated from
Mexico to the United States at the age of 13.
Since then, he has written and published a
book of poetry, *Estranged by the Airfields of
Vienna.* Fran's creative work is mostly
comprised of short prose and free verse. As
an immigrant, his endeavors are based on an
outside-looking-in perspective. Fran is the

183

art editor for *poeticdiversity*, and has been writing poetry for more than 10 years. He lives in Long Beach, California.

**Melanie Gonzalez** is a senior at Eagle Rock High who hopes to be on a banned book list someday.

**Wendy Grosskopf** is a creative writing student at California State University, Northridge. Her work has appeared in *The Moorpark Review* as well as in several online publications. She has recently completed her first book of poems, *Primitive Art*.

**Erik Haber** was born, raised, and corrupted in Los Angeles, California, where he continues to reside. He is a regular on the L.A./Santa Monica open mic scene and hopes to one day be paid for being himself.

**David Herrle** is a working Pittsburgh writer, editor of *SubtleTea*, and aspiring zombie hunter (if an apocalypse of The Undead ever happens.)

Poet/actor/singer **Elizabeth Iannaci** currently serves as co-director of the Valley Contemporary Poets, hosts a monthly reading series for them, and has two

chapbooks of poetry, *Passions Casualties* and the forthcoming *Renoir's Daughter*.
Her work can be found in various publications including Tebot Bach's Anthology of California Poets, *So Luminous the Wildflowers*; *Invisible Planes A Collection To and About Saints, Angels & Deities*; *Angel City Review*; and *Moondance*.
She edits the VCP's yearly anthology, *Beyond the Valley of the Contemporary Poets*, assists at the annual Idyllwild Summer Poetry Festival, and has appeared at countless California venues. Recently she returned from Paris where she read her work at Cité Universitaire for World Poetry Days. She has one son and a picture of a dog.

**Gene Justice** is an American ex-patriate, currently living in South Korea. He is one of the editors, and sometimes a writer, at *Triplopia* (http://www.triplopia.org).

**Rachel Kann,** *L.A. Weekly* award winner and youth poetry workshop leader, performs in L.A. venues from California Plaza to Disney Concert Hall and tours (inter)nationally. She is the creator of co-lab:oration and appears on compilations like *85 Decibel Monks* and in anthologies like *So Luminous The Wildflowers* (Tebot Bach Press) and *L.A. Melange: the first*

185

*year of poeticdiversity* (Sybaritic Press 2004.)
She wants you to come visit her at inspirachel.com

**Marie Lecrivain** is the executive editor of
*poeticdiversity: the litzine of Los Angeles*. She's
a 2nd-level denizen of Dante's *Inferno*, and is
a writer in residence at her apartment.
Her prose and poetry have appeared in *AE
Magazine, Animus, Earth's Daughters, Subtle
Tea, Triplopia,* and in the anthology *L.A
Melange: the first year of poeticdiversity*
(Sybaritic Press 2004). She is the author of
two poetry collections: *Canticle of a Bored
Hausfrau* (Sybaritic Press 2003), and *poetry
whored,* an e-chapbook (Tamafyhr Mountain
Press 2004).
Marie's avocations include photography, Sean
Bean, felines, expensive handbags, and
sensual tributes upon her neck from male
artists-except male poets, who only write
about it.

**Laura A. Lionello** is originally from Chicago,
and the poetry editor for *poeticdiversity.* Her
work has been published in *A Galaxy of
Verse, Anthology, Celebration, green room
confessionals, Penumbra, Portland Review, The
Blue House,* and *Threshold.* She has featured
at the ReallyBigShow/*poeticdiversity* second
BIG, DAMNED POETRY-PACKED reading

(04/04), The Rapp Saloon (12/03), Woman's Words showcase (10/03), and others. Several of her poet friends honored her by reading her work at Our Poetic Voices (08/04). Her poem *Corpse Pose* won a Finalist prize in the 2004 TWA Penumbra Poetry & Haiku Contest.

**Harold Lorin** is just now trying to write poetry and fiction. His recent forays can be found on-line at *Seismic Fish* (www.seismicfish.com), *Nice Stories* (www.nicestories.com) and *The Blue House*. He's published numerous books and articles in Computer Technology and Science. He lives primarily in New York City.

Lorin travels extensively for work and pleasure, thinks truth lies only in fiction (although there are good moments for reconstructionist historians), and is still trying to develop a personal experiment to test if the world is round.

His favorite poets are are Billy Collins, Mark Strand, W.S. Merwin, Elizabeth Bishop, Wallace Stevens, Alfred Tennyson, and John Milton. Otherwise he is "only an aging American who knows little of life."

**Rick Lupert** has been involved in the Los Angeles poetry community since 1990. He served for two years as a co-director of the Valley Contemporary Poets, a 24-year-old non-profit organization that produces a regular reading series and publications out of the San Fernando Valley. His poetry has appeared in numerous magazines and literary journals, including *The Los Angeles Times*, *Chiron Review*, *Zuzu's Petals*, *Caffeine Magazine*, *Blue Satellite*, and others. He is the author of nine books: *Paris: It's the Cheese*, *I Am My Own Orange County*, *Mowing Fargo*, *I'm a Jew. Are You?*, *Stolen Mummies* (Ain't Got No Press), *Lizard King of the Laundromat*, *Brendan Constantine is My Kind of Town* (Inevitable Press), *Feeding Holy Cats*, and *Up Liberty's Skirt* (Cassowary Press).

He serves on the Artist and Community Advisory Council of Beyond Baroque Literary Arts Center in Venice. (though he's not sure how that happened or what it means). He has hosted the long running Cobalt Café reading series in Canoga Park since 1994 and is regularly featured at venues throughout Southern California.

Rick created and maintains the *Poetry Super Highway*, a major Internet resource for poets.

Currently, Rick works as a music teacher at Temple Ahavat Shalom in Northridge and the Valley Cities Jewish Community Center in Van Nuys, as well as at Hillel of Pierce

and Valley Colleges as the Assistant
Director.

**Stosh Machek** is from Chicago, where, he is
fond of saying, "Poetry gets written like car
crashes, and then read like houses on fire."
Before moving to L.A. three years ago, Stosh
would read his poetry to enthusiastic and/
or drunken audiences at venues around
Chicago three to four times a week. He was
a regular reader at Weeds, Floetry at the
Subterranean, and The Green Mill. He also
ran a couple of his own poetry venues:
Wednesday Nites at Cafe Bolero and The
Poetry Thugs. Recently, Stosh has been
hosting The Brand Booksop Poetry & Stories
Reading, a showcase venue at the Brand
Bookshop in Glendale, CA.
He claims that his father was a cinder block, his
mother was a ragged Freudian impulse, and
that his grandmother was a stewardess on
the Luftwaffe.

**Greggory Moore** is a SoCal resident, a civil
libertarian and a copy editor for *Skratch
Magazine*. His short story, "I Dream of
Bicycles," is a section of his recently-
completed first novel, *Story Telling of Death
and So Many Other Things*.

**Craig Murry**'s work has appeared in numerous online and print publications, and has been nominated for the 2004 Pushcart Awards. When Craig is not writing, he is the Architectural Designer for a Conservation Authority as well as an Officer in the Canadian Forces (Reserves).

His first novel, *The Banshee* is being released later this year.

**Leslie Maryann Neal** is the author of two books: *I Want to Be a Bad Girl* and *Paper-Thin Hearts*. In 2004, she recorded a spoken-word CD called *Mermaid.*

**Dave Nordling** is co-host of the Rapp Saloon in Santa Monica, California and the editor-in-chief of Off-World Publications, a small chapbook service for poets.

He has been featured at open-mics and poetry showcases throughout Los Angeles including the Cobalt Cafe, Midnight Special Bookstore, The UnUrban's ReallyBigShow, and the Rapp Saloon. His work has appeared in *Confused in a Deeper Way, The Blue House, PlanetMag, Dufus* and *Unlikely Stories.* He has contributed to various anthologies including *L.A. Melange: the first year of poeticdiversity* (Sybaritic Press 2004), *everything about you is beautiful, green room*

*confessionals, Poets of Midnight,* and *Cracked Pavement & Plastic Trees: Our Gifts to Future Generations.*
He is the author of *From the Blue Folder,* and an upcoming chapbook *Glass Houses* to be released early in 2006.

**Aire Celeste Norell** is a compassionate warrior for peace toward all living things. She is a contributing editor for *poeticdiversity,* while her day job is working with children.
Her work has appeared in *The Blue House* and *San Gabriel Valley Poetry Quarterly.* In 2004 she put together her first poetry chapbook, *The Ugly Duckling & Other American Tragedies.* In the same year, she edited and published an anthology (on tree-free paper using soy ink) of environmental poetry, *Cracked Pavement & Plastic Trees: Our Gifts To Future Generations.* At the top of her list of unfinished projects is writing a contemporary political thriller.
Aire has performed as a featured poet at a number of readings across L.A. and Orange County. She is also guilty of compulsively organizing poetry/music/dance events for good causes. For information about her upcoming scheduled appearances, as well as to read more of her work, please visit her website at: www.aireceleste.com.

**Charlotte O'Brien** was born in England and
lived in Australia and San Francisco before
moving to Los Angeles. She currently
resides in Redondo Beach with her six-year-
old daughter.

Charlotte holds a BA in Creative Art with a
double major in Creative Writing from
Griffith University, and won the Australian
Dorothy Crawford Memorial Scholarship for
Creative Writing. She recently completed the
Master Poetry Class at USC and returned
from Prague where she studied poetry at
Charles University through the USC
program of Professional Writing.

Charlotte is a former co-host for *Feminist
Magazine* on KPFK and a performer and staff
writer for LitRave. Her poetry is published
in journals such as *The Southern Californian
Poetry Anthology* and *Beyond the Valley of the
Contemporary Poets*.

**Angel Uriel Perales** was born in Rio Piedras,
Puerto Rico, and moved to Nashville,
Tennessee at the age of eleven. He holds a
B.A. in English and a B.F.A. in Theatre from
the University of Louisville and another
B.F.A. in Filmmaking from the North
Carolina School of the Arts.

His most recent publications include poems and

short stories that appeared in *Poetry Super
Highway*, *The Thinker*, *Framed*, *Lily*, and *Open
Street Review*, among others. He has written
two collections of poetry and lyrical prose,
*Brown Recluse* (Rumrazor Press, 2002, 97
pages) and *Long* (Rumrazor Press, 2005, 87
pages).

He has worked for Hard Copy, Entertainment
Tonight, and Paramount Pictures. He
currently lives in Studio City and works for
a network affiliated news station in the L.A.
market.

**Alice Pero**'s poetry has been published in many
magazines and anthologies, including *Three
Mile Harbor*, *Salonika*, *San Gabriel Valley Poets
Quarterly*, *The California Poetry Calendar*,
*Word Thursday*, *Trés di-verse-city*, *Albatross*,
*Lummox*, and *The California Quarterly*. She
can be found online at
www.jacketmagazine.com among others.

Alice's first book of poetry, *Thawed Stars*,
published in 1999, was hailed by Kenneth
Koch as having "clarity" and "surprises."
She has won two poetry prizes from the
National League of American Pen Women,
an award from The California State Poetry
Society, and awards from the *San Gabriel
Poetry Quarterly*. *Thawed Stars* is available on
amazon.com or directly from the author at

her website.

Alice has taught poetry to children in private and public schools for 12 years and is a member of the CA Poets in the Schools. In October 2002 she founded a new poetry reading series in Santa Monica, Moonday, which she runs with her co-host, Anne Silver. More information on www.home.earthlink.net/~pero/.

**Brenda Petrakos** is a writer and actress who has been performing in the L.A. spoken word scene for four years.

Her prose has been published in *Dramatist Guild*, *The Messenger*, *The Sylvain*, and in the Really Big Show anthology, *everything about you is beautiful*. Her first play, *Parosia*, received the Dramatist Guild Award.

Brenda's collection, *Quirk & Smirk Stories*, will be performed by the Cult of the Rose Ensemble later this year. Her current work in progress, *Tia's Kitchen*, will be performed as a solo piece in Spring 2006.

**James Pinkerton** has a BA in English from California State University, Northridge. He has worked as a AmeriCorps volunteer coordinator for Habitat for Humanity, college math tutor, substitute elementary school teacher, and pizza delivery man.

James lives in Sunland.

**Douglas Richardson** is the prose editor for
   *poeticdiversity*.
His work has appeared in *The Blue House*,
   *Aesthetica*, and in the anthologies *green room*
   *confessionals, everything about you is beautiful*,
   and *L.A. Melange: the first year of*
   *poeticdiversity* (Sybaritic Press 2004).
Doug  has begun work on a novel, which he
   hopes to complete in 2006.

**Sam Skow** has performed under a few different
   aliases, the most notorious being Barnabus
   Briefchatter and Buddha Hat. As Barnabus
   Briefchatter, Sam's work was published in
   Lydia Lunch's online publication *Sex and*
   *Guts Magazine*. Buddha Hat was a member
   of the 2003 Los Angeles Slam Team, which
   took home the national championship that
   year.
All of this is irrelevant, though, because Sam
   denounces everything that he has ever
   written prior to his latest (only) chapbook
   *Fighting Cancer with Coughdrops*.

**Wanda Vanhoy Smith** was born in Portland,
   Oregon. She has had a children's book
   published by Charles Scribner's Sons. Her
   poetry has been published in several

anthologies including the *Northridge Review* and *Kerf* at College of the Redwoods. She reads poetry at Southern California coffee houses. She has been featured at Coffee Cartel, Sacred Grounds, The Ugly Mug, and Borders Bookstore.

**Kate Soto** lives and writes in Los Angeles. She has a BA in Literature & Italian from UC Santa Cruz and is currently working on an MFA at Antioch University.

**Mark Taylor** currently serves as a southern California city commissioner. In addition to his writing endeavors, Mark is also a professional musician and songwriter. Upon returning to the US after spending two years in Australia, Mark taught computer information systems technology at the community college level for over twelve years.

**Gregory T. Young** is originally from Salem, MA, grew up in Cape Breton Island, in Nova Scotia, and has lived in Los Angeles for about 13 years.

Printed in the United States
40154LVS00001B/1-144

9 780971 223271